Thinking About Death and Immortality

Thinking About Death and Immortality

Paul Badham

Fortress Press

Minneapolis

THINKING ABOUT DEATH AND IMMORTALITY

Fortress Press Edition © 2015
Copyright © Paul Badham 2013

This book is published in cooperation with Society for Promoting Christian Knowledge, London, England. Originally titled *Making Sense of Death and Immortality*. Interior contents have not been changed.

All rights reserved. Except for brief quotations in critical articles or reviews, no part of this book may be reproduced in any manner without prior written permission from the publisher. Visit http://www.augsburgfortress.org/copyrights/contact.asp or write to Permissions, Augsburg Fortress, Box 1209, Minneapolis, MN 55440.

Extracts from the Authorized Version of the Bible (The King James Bible), the rights in which are vested in the Crown, are reproduced by permission of the Crown's Patentee, Cambridge University Press.

Extracts marked REB are from the Revised English Bible and are copyright © Oxford University Press and Cambridge University Press 1989.

Scripture quotations marked RSV are from the Revised Standard Version of the Bible and are copyright © 1946, 1952 and 1971 by the Division of Christian Education of the National Council of the Churches of Christ in the USA. Used by permission. All rights reserved.

Extracts from The Book of Common Prayer, the rights in which are vested in the Crown, are reproduced by permission of the Crown's Patentee, Cambridge University Press.

Library of Congress Cataloging-in-Publication Data
Print ISBN: 978-1-5064-0066-2
eBook ISBN: 978-1-5064-0096-9

The paper used in this publication meets the minimum requirements of American National Standard for Information Services—Permanence of Paper for Printed Library Materials, ANSIZ329.48-1984.

Manufactured in the U.S.A.

*To my clear wife Linda
whose incisive analysis has been invaluable
in sharpening my thinking*

Contents

Introduction		ix
1	Making sense of death	1
2	Making sense of immortality	14
3	The religious context of belief in a future life	25
4	A historical argument for belief in the resurrection of Jesus	37
5	The evidential and religious value of near-death experiences	47
6	Moral and religious arguments against belief in hell	58
7	Concepts of heaven	68
Notes		78

Introduction

For some Christians, belief in life after death has simply evaporated. In part this is due to the overwhelming dominance in our society of a naturalistic interpretation of reality. But also, traditional ways of articulating Christian belief are no longer found helpful. This book is intended to grapple with these issues and to explore arguments for Christian hope today.

Chapter 1 discusses how advances in scientific and medical understanding of the physical basis of personality have influenced belief in life after death. I consider challenges to faith from analytical philosophy and from modern astronomical findings about the vastness of the universe. I also show how evolutionary theory shows us to be part of the natural order. This naturalistic vision is not solely modern. Ancient Israel saw life as having of necessity a natural span. Today, far more of us are likely to live out this span, and this has affected psychological attitudes towards death and dying.

In the second chapter I show how life after death has been central to Christian doctrine, mission and worship. I argue that resurrection and immortality need each other and that both can be defended. I respond to the objections of analytical philosophy and argue that a contemporary dualism of mind and body can fully accept all that modern science tells us about the ways our thoughts and feelings are correlated with physical factors. A strong case for the soul is made on the basis of human free will, religious experiences and near-death experiences.

In Chapter 3 I explore the religious context, starting with how belief in God is consistent with modern physics and noting a revival of interest in the philosophy of religion. I discuss the problem of evil and suggest that life after death is contingent on belief

Introduction

in a Creator God who loves human beings. That people can have a relationship with God is confirmed by religious experience which appears to be a worldwide phenomenon.

Chapter 4 presents the historical evidence for the resurrection of Jesus that gave birth to Christianity and to the distinctively Christian case for a future life. Secular historical sources confirm that Jesus' disciples were so convinced that he had conquered death, they persuaded others to share this extraordinary belief and were themselves prepared to die as witnesses to it. If Jesus had in fact appeared to his disciples, then all these developments are explicable. Without it, the birth of Christianity becomes a complete mystery. I go on to explore the ways in which the resurrection of Jesus has been understood and argue for an interpretation that is relevant to what we can hope for our own future destiny.

Chapter 5 explores the significance of near-death experiences (NDEs) for religious belief. Naturalistic explanations for NDEs are described and their limitations explored. The primary evidential feature of NDEs is the apparent correctness of observations allegedly made from outside the body. I show that NDEs are described in many religious traditions.

Chapter 6 spells out the horror of belief in hell and what it actually meant to people in past ages. I show why the moral conscience of humanity is revolted by this belief and why mainstream churches have in practice ceased to defend such notions. One important element in this chapter is the discussion of the New Testament and the priority given by Jesus to his message of love and forgiveness.

My final chapter considers heaven. As a result of the Copernican revolution, it has become impossible to locate heaven in the sky immediately above the earth. Alternative interpretations are discussed. The first is that God will bring history to an end and create a new world. Another suggests that God alone has immortality and after death we will live eternally in the mind of

Introduction

God. A third interpretation suggests that at death, we pass from time into eternity and eternal repose. This is contrasted with an interpretation based on the life of the world to come, in which individuals will continue to develop.

1
Making sense of death

A naturalistic view of death

From a naturalistic understanding of what makes us human, death means personal extinction. The basic reason for this is that everything that makes us the kind of people we are seems bound up with our physical embodiment. Our thinking, feeling and willing are related to particular brain states which neurophysiologists are increasingly able to identify. Our temperamental type, our character, imagination and intelligence are genetically linked, and the effective working of our endocrine system is essential for our intellectual and emotional well-being. In the light of such considerations, many think that belief in life after death flies in the face of what science has discovered.

> Many think that belief in life after death flies in the face of what science has discovered

Modern scientific knowledge is quantifying, confirming and in some cases extending what experience has taught us for generations. More than 200 years ago David Hume argued: 'the weakness of the body and that of the mind in infancy are exactly proportioned; their vigour in manhood, their sympathetic disorder in sickness; their common gradual decay in old age. The step further seems unavoidable; their common dissolution in death.'[1]

Old Testament perspectives

As we shall see in the next chapter, this naturalistic and mortalist view of human beings is very different from the world-view of historic Christianity. However, it is not solely a post-Enlightenment or modern perspective. The proposition 'all men are mortal' was seen in ancient Greek philosophy as the classic example of a logical truism. The use of the phrase 'to expire' as a synonym for death reflects the belief that when a person breathes out for the last time then that person ceases to be. It seems that this is also how we should understand biblical phrases about the spirit returning to God who gave it. Although within the Christian tradition such expressions have often been interpreted as a reference to the 'parting of soul and body at death', the consensus of Old Testament scholarship is that it refers to God taking back his own life-sustaining spirit. The Hebrew word for spirit, *ruah*, is best understood as 'breath', and the Hebrew word *nepes*, though often translated as 'soul' actually means 'life'. So when we are told that Rachel's *nepes* departed, this simply means that she died.[2] The Hebrew does not mean that her soul left her, as if it were something that could go off on its own. The Hebrew Bible, just as much as modern biology, sees human beings as irreducibly part of the natural order.

> The Hebrew Bible, just as much as modern biology, sees human beings as irreducibly part of the natural order

Heart, kidneys, bowels, liver, inward parts, flesh and bones are all explicitly mentioned in the Old Testament as shaping and determining our character and emotions.[3] According to the Psalmist, human beings are like the beasts that perish, the grass that withers and the flowers that fade.[4] In the presence of death, Job thinks that we are less fortunate than the plants, for 'if a tree is cut down, there is hope that it will sprout again . . . But when a human being dies all his power vanishes.'[5] In ancient Hebrew thought, God's enduring covenant was with the whole people of Israel, not with individuals whose deaths were simply part of the ongoing cycle of life.

Making sense of death

Given this perspective, Ecclesiastes argues that human life can have no ultimate meaning and therefore in the language of the King James Bible he speaks of life as 'vanity of vanities; all is vanity'. Modern translations prefer to talk of 'emptiness' or 'futility'. Ecclesiastes thought that although life could have no ultimate purpose, we should not despair but should find fulfilment in the limited goals open to us within our mortal existence, believing that

> there is nothing good for anyone except to be happy and live the best life he can while he is alive ... It is good and proper for a man to eat and drink and enjoy himself in return for his labours ... Enjoy life with a woman you love all the days of your allotted span here under the sun ... Whatever task lies to your hand, do it with might; because [in the grave to which you are heading], there is neither doing nor thinking.[6]

Evolution and our place in the natural order

Over the past 150 years, the naturalistic case for extinction has been strengthened by the way that evolution shows the place of human beings within the natural order. Like other developed animals, we evolved over millions of years, and over many generations *homo sapiens* gradually emerged from earlier forms of life. Modern genetic studies further strengthen this picture by revealing that the vast majority of our genetic inheritance is shared with other species. Like them, our development has been shaped by the struggle for existence. In our case, as in theirs, death has played a crucial role in our progressive adaptation to the challenges of existence. Without death there could have been no progress. The qualities we value in life reflect an awareness of our finitude and our lives find their meaning as the various stages of life offer opportunities for our personal development. If medical research were ever to discover how to reverse the

> An 'elixir of immortality' is an age-old fantasy, but its actual realization would be a disaster

ageing process, humanity would be faced with appalling choices. An 'elixir of immortality' is an age-old fantasy. Its actual realization would be a disaster. Human society depends on each generation passing away and handing on the baton to their successors.

Evolutionary difficulties in relation to immortality

Although Darwin did not think that his findings affected the validity of belief in a Creator God, he recognized from an early stage that they challenged belief in the immortality of the soul.[7] He was right to do so. As I have sought to show elsewhere, in my article 'Do animals have immortal souls?', the Christian tradition has held that of all God's creatures, only human beings are heirs of eternal life.[8] Though animals are distinguished from plant life through their possession of a sentient soul (*anima* is the Latin word for soul), traditional belief holds that this kind of soul is mortal. It was not thought intelligible to suppose that animals have the kind of consciousness that could conceivably exist without a body. Aquinas was clear that even for humans, the existence of self-aware consciousness in a disembodied state could only be a temporary stage in the transition to an eternal life.[9] However, the belief that human beings are fundamentally different from other animals, as tradition has taught, now faces the serious objection that there are no sudden breaks in the evolutionary pathway leading to *homo sapiens*.

> There are no sudden breaks in the evolutionary pathway leading to *homo sapiens*

Linda Badham argues:

> somewhere along that line we might feel reasonably secure in denying that such and such a creature had any self awareness whereas most normal adult humans do possess such an awareness. But between these extremes lies a grey area. To have a non-arbitrary dividing

line it has to be possible, for us to decide at least in principle, where a sharp division can be drawn between the last generation of anthropoid apes and the first generation of true homo sapiens? Are we to suppose that . . . the changes between one generation and the next were so great that the children counted in God's eyes as the bearers of immortality while their parents were 'mere animals'?[10]

Moreover, suppose an older 'ape-like' hominid married one of the new generation 'humans'. How could the one enjoy immortality knowing that the other had perished for ever? Simply to state the predicament is to indicate its unsatisfactoriness. This difficulty is compounded by recent discoveries that there may have been as many as six different species of humanity coexisting for long periods of time and possibly even interbreeding with one another. It is also likely that for the first three million years that human beings lived on earth our lives were virtually indistinguishable from those of other animals. Those features of civilization that most differentiate us go back fewer than 10,000 years.

The problem of when personal life begins

The difficulty of saying when distinctively human life emerged is recapitulated when we consider the comparable impossibility of identifying when personal life begins in any individual today. Clearly there is a sense in which my distinctive identity goes back to the moment of conception, for at that point my unique DNA code came into existence. Yet 70 per cent of zygotes develop no further than this initial stage, and are expelled from the mother's body as foetal wastage in what she experiences as simply a late menstrual period.[11] It would be wholly unintelligible to imagine that 70 per cent of the future population of 'heaven' should be unformed zygotes! The moment of implantation will not do either, since we would then face the difficulty of identical twins whose separation may well take place after implantation and we can hardly suppose that a 'person' splits into two up to four weeks after beginning life. 'Animation' is equally problematic, as the timing of a baby's first movement being reported depends more on the mother's subjective interpretation of what is going on in her womb rather than on any clearly identifiable development in the child. The fact simply is that 'somewhere' in the path leading from conception to adulthood, consciousness comes into being, but it is impossible to draw dividing lines in what is a seamlessly continuous process.

> 'Somewhere' in the path leading from conception to adulthood, consciousness comes into being in what is a seamlessly continuous process

The logic of mortality

Consideration of the place of human beings in the natural order has led many contemporary philosophers to the conclusion that the possibility of personal life after bodily death is literally 'non sense'. Wittgenstein alerted his contemporaries to the danger of ignoring the everyday use of the language we speak, and the context in which we learnt to utter the words we use. He believed that if we paid attention to the meaning of the words involved, we would realize that 'death is not lived through' and that 'the world in death does not change but ceases'.[12] Antony Flew developed this argument further, coining the slogan 'people are what you meet' and pointing out that what we do meet are creatures of flesh and blood who can be pointed at, touched, heard, seen and talked to. 'Person words refer to people. And how can such objects as people survive physical dissolution?'[13]

The size and age of the universe

Further difficulties for the Christian valuation of human beings come from the growing realization of our utter insignificance in cosmic terms. The early Christians believed that this earth had been directly created by God in the relatively recent past for the benefit of human beings. With heaven above and the underworld below, it constituted the whole of reality. The sun, moon and stars existed to provide us with light, while plants and animals existed to provide us with food. In this context it was natural to believe that people mattered to their Creator and that he would not wish death to be their final end.

> Further difficulties for the Christian valuation of human beings come from the growing realization of our utter insignificance in cosmic terms

For a contemporary person, the world-view is very different. To clarify how great the difference is, I give the numbers involved in full because I am aware that the similarity in sound between 'million' and 'billion' can often obscure the difference between them. The fact is that the universe as we know it is at least 12 hundred thousand million years old. Our galaxy alone contains at least one hundred thousand million other stars and there are at least one hundred thousand million other galaxies. Although the conditions under which life can develop are relatively rare, astronomers are daily finding planets in other solar systems. At least some of these planets are orbiting around their stars in the 'Goldilocks' position of being neither too cold, nor too hot, but 'just right' for life to evolve. There may well be eight hundred million such planets in our own galaxy, even though the distances involved rule out our ever meeting their inhabitants. Logically speaking, such considerations need not affect Christian confidence that each of us matters eternally to our Creator; but psychologically they do tend to erode such confidence.

The human life span

Human beings, like other evolved creatures, have a natural lifespan. The classic description of this appears in Psalm 90 in the Book of Common Prayer:

> The days of our age are threescore years and ten;
> and though men be so strong that they come to fourscore years:
> yet is their strength then but labour and sorrow;
> so soon passeth it away, and we are gone.

What this tells us is that for the past 3,000 years or so it has been the human experience that, if we do not succumb earlier to accident or disease, we can usually expect to live to our seventies, and the stronger among us can live on into our eighties. But after we get into our eighties life is very much a struggle, and for most elderly people their eighties prove to be a fatal decade. There have always been a few who have lived on into their nineties and hundreds. In the Bible, after the obviously mythological lifespans attributed to patriarchs like Methuselah, we are told that God made 'a hundred and twenty years' the upper limit for any human existence.[14] This is the foundation for the traditional Jewish blessing, 'May you live to be a hundred and twenty.' However, Jeanne Calment is the only documented case of a person who actually reached 120. She died in 1997 at the age of 122. The oldest person alive in 2012 was 116. Talk of ever-increasing absolute longevity is not supported by reality.[15]

The coming of a 'third age'

What has changed in human experience is not the existence of old age, but that the majority of us in the developed world can reasonably expect to live to see it. No longer do half of children die before the age of five. No longer is giving birth profoundly life-threatening to women, and no longer will most of us succumb to infectious disease in mid-life. Whereas in sixteenth-century London only 5 per cent lived on into their seventies, by 1998 75 per cent did so. Global life expectancy jumped from 30 to 67 years during the nineteenth and twentieth centuries.[16] According to HSBC airport posters, two-thirds of all human beings who have reached the age of 65 are alive today.

The majority of us can now look forward to a 'third age' of life after we have finished with work. If we are reasonably fortunate, we may enjoy a life of leisure, albeit followed in due course by a period of terminal illness. This is a very new phenomenon. In 1948 a man was lucky if he lived to collect his pension, for the average age of death for a man was 65.[17] By contrast, according to the Office of National Statistics website in 2010, a man who reached 65 in 2010 could on average expect to have a further 9.9 years of healthy life followed in due course by 6.5 years of ill health, of which the final 3.9 years would be increasingly restricted by illness. Between 1991 and 2001 average life expectancy rose by 2.2 years, but unfortunately only 0.6 were years of health. The other 1.6 extra years were years of persistent illness.[18]

> Two-thirds of all human beings who have reached the age of 65 are alive today

Holding death at bay

An important feature of modern medicine is our ability to hold death at bay even when hope of cure is long gone. For example, people with respiratory disease can be provided with oxygen. Linked by a kind of umbilical cord to their oxygen generator, sufferers with breathing difficulties can enjoy a year or two of additional life in their own homes, while motorized scooters can provide independence and mobility long after walking has become impossible. Likewise, pills to prevent water retention, lower blood cholesterol, and to reduce blood pressure can all help in the fight against heart disease. New cancer treatments can sometimes cure and will frequently enable people to live with the disease for several years beyond when it would have killed them in the past. Pneumonia, formerly known as 'the old man's friend', need no

Making sense of death

longer release him from this life for it can be treated by antibiotics, as can many other formerly fatal infections.

In hospitals death can, of course, be kept further at bay by saline drips and respirators, not to mention kidney dialysis, organ transplantation, and heart bypass operations. If a person's heart stops beating in an intensive therapy unit, every possible effort may be made at resuscitation, and it is not unknown for this process to be repeated many times before death becomes impossible to resist any longer. In general a host of new technologies and a cornucopia of new drugs can nowadays keep life in being long beyond anything possible in the past. It is even possible to use life-support systems to keep a person's body functioning for years after they have lost all consciousness. The former Israeli Prime Minister Ariel Sharon entered a persistent vegetative state on 4 January 2006, and at the time of writing, more than six and half years later, he was still in that condition. According to *Le Monde*, his round-the-clock clinical care costs €300,000 (£238,000) a year. In Sharon's case this is largely paid for by a grateful state, but clearly no health service could survive if it allowed such support to be widely available.[19]

Changing attitudes to death

Growing awareness and experience of the implications of the 'third age' have profoundly affected people's attitude to death and immortality. The extension of most people's lives into the seventies and eighties means that more and more of us feel that we have lived out our natural span. As a consequence, belief in a future life has tended to evaporate. Historically, a powerful psychological factor in wanting to believe in a life after death was

> Growing awareness and experience of the implications of the 'third age' have profoundly affected people's attitude to death and immortality

the unsatisfactoriness of lives cut short before people had had the opportunity to discharge their family responsibilities, fully develop their character or to achieve the goals they had set themselves. This remains the way that death is seen concerning those struck down prematurely, whether in infancy or in the prime of life. For them, death is still responsible for 'cutting short' the natural span of life, and is considered the worst thing that could happen to anyone because it deprives a person of all the potential life still had to offer. However, for those who die after many years of retirement, the situation is different. They know what they have been able to accomplish during their lives and may have no further major goals ahead. Consequently, some people in their eighties seem content to accept that their existence will come to a natural end.

Changing attitudes to dying

Historically, death usually came relatively swiftly, in days or weeks rather than years. This can still happen and when it does it is experienced as particularly tragic. However, for those who survive into old age, the fear of death has been for some replaced by the fear of being kept alive beyond sense and reason. Douglas Davies, in his *Brief History of Death*, talks movingly of the 'national nursing home scenario' in which post-80-year-olds live lonely lives 'deprived of those active commitments and obligations to others that make life worthwhile'.[20]

> The stock nightmare of modern times is of doctors in possession of the power to keep us alive when our bodies are at least partly dead

In their *A Good Death: Conversations with East Londoners*, Michael Young and Lesley Cullen found that 'the stock nightmare of modern times is of doctors in possession of the power to keep us alive when our bodies are at least partly dead'.

This prospect is 'more frightening than the prospect of being killed'.[21] Many people have witnessed the lengthy and distressing dying process of a close relative. It is factors like these that lie behind the existence of societies like Dignity in Dying, which supports moves to legalize assisted dying.

The challenge of the naturalistic understanding

The dominance of a naturalistic understanding of life is the primary reason why the idea of life after death is simply a nonstarter for many secular thinkers. It also explains why some, while nominally affirming a future hope, have no lively expectation of its realization. Many committed Christians suffer 'cognitive dissonance' through awareness of how much their faith differs from the secular assumptions that dominate contemporary discussion. It is hard to continue to believe in something that contradicts the 'common sense' of the contemporary world-view. I sometimes feel haunted by the challenge of Francis Crick to those who continue to believe in the soul: 'What everyone believed yesterday, and you believe today, only cranks will believe tomorrow.'[22] It worries me because during my academic lifetime there has been an increasing tendency for neuroscientists and philosophers to take for granted a materialist view of the mind. Back in 1966, 22 of the world's leading neurophysiologists contributed to Sir John Eccles' edited book, *The Brain and Conscious Experience*. They were united in *insisting* that no materialist theory could account for the workings of the human brain. This would not be true of the leading neuroscientists of today. Similarly in philosophy: when D. M. Armstrong's book *A Materialist Theory of Mind* was published in 1968 it was dismissed by many philosophers

> Materialism has moved from being an antipodean heresy to being the contemporary orthodoxy

as 'the Australian heresy', because both D. M. Armstrong and J. J. C. Smart came from that continent. But since then, materialism has moved from being an Antipodean heresy to being the contemporary orthodoxy.

To succeed in 'making sense of immortality', one must not only show why the Christian hope matters, but also how the challenge of this naturalistic world-view can be met.

2
Making sense of immortality

Christianity as a religion of salvation

Christianity came into being as a religion of salvation offering the assurance of eternal life after death. According to 1 Peter 1.3–4, 'we have been born anew to a living hope through the resurrection of Jesus Christ from the dead, and to an inheritance which is imperishable, undefiled, and unfading, kept in heaven for you' (RSV). Life after death was so integral to St Paul's understanding of the Christian message that he thought that without it 'faith was futile'. One could carry on quoting such texts almost indefinitely, for 'belief in a future world is taken for granted' in all the New Testament documents.[1] It was their absolute faith in a life beyond that enabled many of the first Christians to embrace martyrdom with composure and even with enthusiasm, and thereby convert those who watched them die in the amphitheatres of the Roman empire. On the mission field it was the hope of immortality that was seen as Christianity's distinctive attraction.

> The hope of immortality was seen as Christianity's distinctive attraction

For example, when the Anglo-Saxons of Northumbria were debating whether or not to accept this new faith, the clinching argument was that on a Christian view, life would no longer be seen as an interlude between two eternal states of darkness, but rather as the prelude to a yet more glorious future.[2]

Life after death: the heart of Christianity

Throughout the Christian centuries, belief in a future life was the heart of all living faith. The great themes of Christian theology – incarnation, atonement, salvation, justification – all revolved around the good news of an eternal hope. This theme was taken up into each of the Christian sacraments. At baptism a Christian is said to be 'an inheritor of the kingdom of heaven', and reference to God's everlasting kingdom is made at the most solemn moments of confirmation, marriage, ordination and absolution. In the Holy Communion service Christians receive 'the bread of immortality' in the Orthodox liturgy, or the bread of 'eternal' or 'everlasting life' in Anglican and Roman formularies. Finally, in the last rites the Christian receives the viaticum to nourish his soul for the journey through death.

This is in no sense an abstract belief. It is this faith that also finds expression in the classic hymns and carols of Easter and in the regular weekly worship of all the Christian churches. Consider, for example, the Easter hymn, 'Jesus lives!'

> Jesus lives! thy terrors now
> can no more, O death, appal us;
> Jesus lives! by this we know
> thou, O grave, canst not enthral us.

Any Easter hymn could be cited to make the same point. What Easter is believed to be about is the conquest of death by Jesus' resurrection. If this belief ceases to be held, the hymns become unintelligible.

The two components of the Christian hope

Historically, Christianity has affirmed both the resurrection of the body and the immortality of the soul.

Both beliefs were taken for granted by the Fathers of the Church, by the medieval schoolmen, the Reformers, and the most recent papal encyclical on the question.[3] But in contemporary theology, the soul is often dismissed as a Greek intrusion into Christian doctrine, while in popular religious thought among the laity resurrection is usually ignored. Yet the two beliefs need each other. The soul, consciousness, or self-awareness must survive bodily death in order to be the bridge between this life and the next. If God simply created a new body suited to a new life in a new world, why should that be of any interest to me if it were not owned by my present personality?

> Christianity has affirmed both the resurrection of the body and the immortality of the soul

Problems with belief in the resurrection of 'this flesh'

In the second century the old Roman Creed affirmed the resurrection of *this* flesh and it became customary at this point to cross oneself to indicate which flesh one was talking about. In the Apostles' Creed this was changed slightly to resurrection of *the* flesh. Cranmer changed this further in the sixteenth century to resurrection of the body as being truer to the New Testament. For subsequent Christians, this latter change had the further advantage of being more open to reinterpretation. However, *The Teaching of Christ: A Catholic Catechism for Adults* affirms that each person will one day rise again 'as the same person he was, in the same flesh made living by the same spirit'.[4] This is the literal belief that was common in early Christianity. Most of the Christian Fathers believed that the 'particles composing each individual's flesh' will be collected together, the 'sea will give up its dead', the cannibal will restore the flesh he has borrowed, and 'the identical structure which death had previously destroyed' will be restored.[5] However, this belief system faces insuperable problems for today. The most obvious is that our bodies are not made up of particles which belong to us.

Our bodies are part of an ever-changing cycle of life. At least 60 per cent of our body weight is water and will have passed through around seven other bodies since it last fell as rain. We have ten times more bacterial cells than human cells within our bodies.[6] Most of us today will die in old age and would certainly not want the identical structure that dies to be restored to us. Moreover, a resurrection body that really was identical to the body that died would immediately die again. Hence we have to posit a different body, healed from all disease, for the notion to make sense. As John Macquarrie argued, a literal resurrection is 'such a remote and bizarre possibility that it is hard to see that it offers much support for belief in a life to come'.[7] Consequently, contemporary discussion of life after death almost always focuses either on the immortality of the soul or on a resurrection that does not entail the resuscitation or re-creation of our present bodies. However, logical problems about the appropriate use of language, raised, for example, by Flew and Wittgenstein, have to be grappled with.

> Our bodies are not made up of particles which belong to us

A reply to linguistic objections to talk of survival of death

It is certainly true that we originally learn person words by reference to our present embodiment. However, there is no reason why this should restrict their wider use. In our childhood, and indeed for most of human history, what was meant by the word 'sun' was a circle of warming light which we observed rising and setting. Its astronomical meaning was something we learnt later. The same is true of almost everything about the world. The world described by science is very different from the world as we experience it in

Making sense of immortality

our lives. As A. J. Ayer says, 'there is no reason why the meaning of words should be indissolubly tied to the context in which they are originally learnt'.[8] If we become aware of new contexts and new realities then we have to extend our language use to cover the new situation. Moreover, Flew is actually wrong when he included the word 'I' in his list of person words. He argued that person words like 'I, you, Flew, father, butcher all refer in one way or another to objects'. But this is not true of the personal pronoun, I, which always relates to me as subject.

Although it is doubtless true that our usage of the personal pronoun was learnt by observing how other people use it of their own public actions, we all subsequently go on to use the word 'I' as the subject of our inward thoughts, feeling or intentions which we alone have access to. For example, I may genuinely feel pain even if, through a stoic response, I conceal this from others. Or again, only I can know what I experience in my dreams and only I can know whether or not I see after-images when I close my eyes.

For any individual, self-identity is constituted by subjective experience. Consider the sci-fi situation as in the TV series *Quantum Leap*. If I discovered that the face I proposed to shave was unfamiliar to me, I would have to conclude that something very odd had happened to my body; but I could not deny that this bizarre event had happened to me if that was how I really did experience it. That persons actually do identify personhood with inner experience is also supported by consideration that we can follow the plot of sci-fi or fairy stories involving a person changing bodies and therefore we cannot say that such stories are unintelligible.

Likewise if we were to experience continuity of consciousness through death, we would accept that we had continued to be even if our consciousness were either disembodied or re-embodied. People who say that while deeply unconscious and near the point of death they went outside their bodies and observed the attempts being made to resuscitate them identify themselves with the observing consciousness rather than with the unconscious body (see Chapter 5).

The point for which I am arguing is that life after death is logically possible if we identify personal continuity in terms of the continuity or restoration of consciousness in a new existence.

> Life after death is logically possible if we identify personal continuity in terms of the continuity or restoration of consciousness in a new existence

I accept that to discuss this possibility entails extending normal language use, but this is legitimate if we are thinking of a possible new reality. As A. J. Ayer commented, 'If there could conceivably be disembodied spirits, the fact that it might not be correct to call them persons would not perhaps be of very great importance.'[9]

Dualism and the physical basis of mind

Descartes' philosophy of dualism is often criticized for claiming that mind and body are totally distinct. However, Descartes insisted on mind–body interaction at all times in normal life. According to Descartes, 'I am not only lodged in my body like a pilot on a ship, but besides I am joined to it very closely and indeed so compounded and intermingled with my body that I form as it were a single whole with it.'[10]

> Mind and brain cannot logically be considered *identical* because some phenomena can only be accounted for if we make a distinction between them

His position was that mind and brain cannot logically be considered *identical* because there are some phenomena that can only be accounted for if we make a distinction between them.

Modern defenders of belief in the soul similarly take for granted the physical basis of personality and the relationships that exist between mental events and brain processes.

The case for the soul

There are three main arguments: free will, religious experiences and near-death experiences. First, we need a concept of the soul to justify our belief in the value of human reasoning and our conviction that we can be responsible for our actions. On a totally materialistic understanding of personhood, all our thoughts and feelings must be the product of antecedent physical causes. As the eighteenth-century philosopher Baron d'Holbach classically put it, 'The brain secretes thought just as the liver secretes bile.'[11] The difficulty with this view is that if this is so, then our sense of purposive rational thought must be an illusion. Jacques Monod, a Nobel prize-winner in 1965 for his researches in biology, argued elsewhere that this is indeed the case. For him, everything is dependent on 'chance and necessity' and hence there can be no such thing as purpose. He did acknowledge, however, that there was 'a radically insoluble . . . flagrant epistemological contradiction' in his believing this and yet continuing to think that his own writing could be goal-directed. He announced that he had chosen to make a 'moral choice' to ignore this internal inconsistency in his reasoning. But one cannot 'choose', as Monod did, to write a book to show that there is no such thing as purpose, because the very act of choosing and indeed writing such a book demonstrates the importance of purpose in human thought, and hence the falsehood of physical determinism.[12] We can only be responsible agents if we are not simply determined by antecedent physical conditions.

Religious experience also challenges materialism. No one believes that religious awareness comes through the senses. Heavenly visions are not the kind of things that cameras can record, and though people may believe that God has 'called them' to particular vocations, no one imagines that a tape recorder could transcribe such a message. If religious experience is treated as evidential because of the impact it has on people's lives, it remains the case that 'spiritual things are spiritually discerned'.[13]

Near-death experiences are another phenomenon that challenges a purely physical interpretation of what it means to be human. Around 25,000 people resuscitated from apparent death have claimed that at the moment their hearts stopped beating 'they' left their bodies and looked down on the resuscitation attempts. Yet if consciousness can come apart from the body, even for only a few seconds near the point of death, the principle has been established that mind and brain are not identical.[14]

The soul as an emergent property

One possible way of reconciling an acknowledgement of the physical basis of our personality with the case for the soul is to suggest that the soul is an emergent property we develop during life. This idea takes literally the idea of this life as a vale of soul-making, as described by John Hick. According to Hick:

> The soul is an emergent property we develop during life

> Distinctive human mentality and spirituality emerges, in accordance with the divine purpose in complex bodily organism. But once it has emerged it is the vehicle, according to Christian faith, of a continuing creative activity, only the beginnings of which have so far taken place.[15]

The difference between mind and brain

According to Richard Swinburne, a dualism of mind and brain is 'inescapable' if we are really to explain human existence and experience. First, he points out that though 'the mental life of thought, sensation and purpose may be caused by physico-chemical events in the brain, it is quite different from them'.[16] Second, he states that 'conscious experiences are causally efficacious. Our thoughts and feelings are not just phenomena caused by goings-on in the brain; they cause other thoughts and feelings and make a difference to the agent's behaviour.' Third, 'though a human soul has a structure and character formed in part through the brain to which it is connected . . . [it] acquires some independence of that brain'.[17] Keith Ward takes a similar line: 'Of course the soul depends on the brain . . . but the soul need not always depend on the brain any more than a man need always depend on the womb which supported his life before birth.'[18]

Twentieth-century Church teaching

Throughout the twentieth century the concept of the soul was one of the most contested within Christian theology. However, the mainstream churches have insisted that belief in the soul remains an essential ingredient of the Christian hope for life after death. In 1938 the Church of England Doctrine Commission declared:

> We ought to reject quite frankly the literalistic belief in a future resuscitation of the actual physical frame which is laid in the tomb. It is to be affirmed nonetheless, that in the life of the world to come the soul or spirit will still have its appropriate organ of expression and activity, which is one with the body of earthly life in the sense that it bears the same relation to the same spiritual entity.[19]

The 1994 *Catechism of the Catholic Church* likewise states that the soul 'is immortal; it does not perish when it separates from the body at death'. In death the 'human body decays and the soul goes to meet God, while awaiting its reunion with its glorified body'.[20]

In 1996 the Church of England Doctrine Commission responded to philosophical criticism of the concept of the soul by adopting a somewhat more nuanced approach:

> It would not be possible to speak of salvation in terms of the destiny of souls after death, if the soul were thought of as the detachable

spiritual part of ourselves. If the essential human being is an embodied whole, our ultimate destiny must be the resurrection and transformation of our entire being... to speak thus is not to abandon talk of the soul, but to seek its redefinition. What the word is needed for is to represent the essential nature which constitutes us in our individual particularities. The essence of humanity is certainly not the matter of the body, for that is continuously changing through wear and tear, eating and drinking. What provides continuity and unity through the flux of change is not material... but the vastly complex information-bearing pattern in which that material is composed. That pattern can surely be considered the carrier of memories and of the personality.

Death 'dissolves the embodiment of that pattern, but the person, whose that pattern is, is "remembered" by God who in love holds that unique being in his care'. However, at some point there must be 'a fuller realisation of God's purpose for us all' which will come with the 'resurrection of the body', though 'it is not to be supposed that the material of the resurrection body is the same as that of old... St Paul warns us "flesh and blood cannot inherit the kingdom of God nor does the perishable inherit the imperishable."'[21]

What is striking about this view is that it recognizes that no realistic belief in a future life today can speak of continuity of material identity, and yet at the same time the Commission acknowledges that the immortality of the soul alone cannot suffice to ensure the future life of persons such as we are. Any belief in a future resurrection, however understood, depends on the continuity through death of something we can call the 'soul' which acts as the bearer of our personhood.

> Belief in a future resurrection depends on the continuity through death of something we can call the 'soul' which acts as the bearer of our personhood

This soul can be understood as an emergent property of our developing personhood through life, or as something that we develop and is held in existence in the mind of God in the way the 1996 Doctrine Commission describes.

Ongoing problems

The crux of the matter is that the concept of the soul is a necessary ingredient of any faith, affirming that we are more than physically determined creatures; that we have the potential for moral and rational growth; and that we can develop a spiritual identity that can ultimately transcend our bodily death. I have tried in this chapter to argue that this remains a belief that can be rationally defended. But I am conscious that difficulties remain.

I cannot be unaware of such difficulties because my wife Linda wrote her doctoral thesis on 'emergence'. In this she argues that emergence is a useful tool to recognize that we need different language-games to distinguish physical and mental qualities of the same material substratum. I recognize also that according to the Open University textbook *Philosophy of Religion*, Linda's essay, 'Problems of Resurrection', provides the definitive case against any belief in a future life.[22] For more than 20 years, I jointly taught courses in death and immortality and the philosophy of religion with Professor David Cockburn. The author of *An Introduction to the Philosophy of Mind*, Professor Cockburn takes a strongly anti-dualist position and we constantly debated these issues.[23] I am therefore well aware that the consensus of twentieth-century philosophy of mind was opposed to dualism, despite the eminence of such philosophers as Hick, Ward and Swinburne whose works I have cited. I thus face a serious problem of 'cognitive dissonance' in continuing to affirm the necessity of the concept of the soul. But I can see no alternative if I am genuinely to affirm the evidential reality of religious experience, human freedom and responsibility, and the hope for a future life.

3
The religious context of belief in a future life

Belief in a Creator God

In Christian doctrine, belief in a future life exists in the context of belief in an all-powerful and all-loving Creator God to whom human beings can relate. Within this belief system life after death is intelligible, whereas within a naturalistic worldview it is not. There are therefore two questions we must address. First, is it reasonable to believe that God exists, and second, is it reasonable to suppose that human beings can relate to God? Jonathan Clatworthy has addressed most issues concerning the first question in another book in this series, *Making Sense of Faith in God*. Hence on the first question, I shall confine myself to the issue of how far Christian belief in God can be judged to be a rational faith within a scientific understanding of reality.

I start with a reminder that all mainstream churches take for granted that evolution is integral to God's creative purposes, so this ought not to be a problem for belief in a Creator God. Darwin himself was clear that his theory was perfectly compatible with belief in a Creator God; in the second and all subsequent editions of *The Origin of Species* he added the words 'by the Creator' to the final summing-up paragraph of his book. Belief in a Creator God is

> Belief in a Creator God is compatible with developments in the natural sciences in the twentieth and twenty-first centuries

The religious context of belief in a future life

even more compatible with developments in the natural sciences in the twentieth and twenty-first centuries.

Today there is a widespread consensus among scientists that the universe has not always existed. It came into being from nothing some 13 thousand million years ago. This does not, of course, prove that God created the universe out of nothing. But the two beliefs are readily compatible with each other. The scientific belief that the universe came into being out of nothing and the Christian belief that God created the universe out of nothing fit very easily together, and it is entirely rational for a person to hold them both.

Similarly there is a scientific consensus that the universe appears to be 'finely tuned' for the emergence of life and mind, since if the conditions just after the big bang had been even fractionally different the universe could not have evolved in the way it has. In his *Brief History of Time* Stephen Hawking showed that the heat of the universe one second after the big bang had to be exactly as it was because a decrease in heat by as little as one part in a million million would have caused the universe to collapse.[1] Similar fine-tuning is necessary for about 50 constants of nature, and this readily lends itself to the idea that there may be a cosmic mind behind all this. But once again, scientific belief in the fine-tuning of the universe does not require belief in God and Hawking is not a believer. All one can legitimately claim is that scientific belief in the fine-tuning of the universe and Christian belief in God as the mind behind the universe go happily together.

This was a phenomenon noted by philosopher Antony Flew, who preceded Richard Dawkins as 'the most notorious atheist in the world'.[2] At an early stage of his 'pilgrimage from atheism to theism',[3] Flew came to think that if a cradle Roman Catholic believes that the universe has a beginning, then acceptance of the big bang 'surely does provide empirical confirmation of . . . that belief'. Likewise if a person believes in a purposeful creation then 'it is entirely reasonable to welcome the fine-tuning argument as providing confirmation of that belief'.[4] Some years later Flew went further than this and in January 2004 announced that he had come to believe in God. He 'simply had to go where the evidence leads', and it seemed to him that the case for God 'is now much stronger than it ever was before'.[5]

The revival of the philosophy of religion

The idea that the case for God is now much stronger can be seen in the way that philosophy of religion has been transformed in the past 50 years. As an undergraduate at Oxford in the early 1960s, I was very conscious that it was regarded as a fringe subject. In theology it was an optional extra rather than part of the normal syllabus. In philosophy the positivistic school led by A. J. Ayer took the view that religious claims were not so much false as meaningless. Since then the situation has radically changed. Professor William Abraham, who arrived in Oxford as a graduate student in 1973, says that he little knew then that he was arriving 'at the beginning of a golden period in the philosophy of religion' in which believers could 'take a lead and create the intellectual space in which Christian belief could be taken seriously once again. The outcome over the last forty years, as seen in the wealth of material that has been published, has been startling in its originality and depth.'[6]

This assessment of a newly confident Christian philosophy in the past 40 years is confirmed by the Canadian atheist philosopher Kai Nielsen.

Writing in 1971, Nielsen said that philosophers who took the claims of religion seriously were 'very much in the minority and their arguments have been forcefully contested'. But nearly 20 years later Nielsen's estimate of philosophical attitudes was quite different:

> Philosophy of religion in Anglo-American context has taken a curious turn in the past decade ... what has come to the forefront ... is

The religious context of belief in a future life

a group of Christian philosophers of a philosophically analytic persuasion, but hostile to even the residues of logical empiricism or Wittgensteinianism, who return to the old topics and the old theses of traditional Christian philosophy and natural theology.[7]

That Nielsen describes this development as 'curious' indicates that he himself remains unconvinced. Nonetheless, it is intriguing that Richard Purtill similarly says of the contemporary debate: 'All the traditional arguments have able and respected defenders, and if there is not a consensus in favour of philosophical arguments for God's existence, it is no longer true that there is a consensus against.'[8]

> If there is not a consensus in favour of philosophical arguments for God's existence, it is no longer true that there is a consensus against

In his introduction to the section on the twentieth century in the five-volume *History of Western Philosophy of Religion*, Professor Charles Taliaferro writes:

> One general observation seems secure: philosophical reflection on religion has formed a major vibrant part of some of the best philosophy in the past century ... At the close of the century there are more societies, institutions, journals, conferences and publishing houses dedicated to philosophy of religion than any other area of philosophy.[9]

It is important not to overstate the case. Arguments about God remain strongly contested and most philosophers are still atheists. The difference between now and 50 years ago is that the arguments are taken seriously. Factors that have changed the situation include the collapse of logical positivism and of atheistic Marxism, together with a distrust of Freudian analysis. Within philosophy an important development has been the recognition that knowledge cannot be simply confined to what we discover through the natural sciences. Disciplines like history, law, literary studies, politics, sociology, aesthetics and philosophy, as well as theology, provide sensible arguments for the support of one theory rather than another even though they cannot provide scientific certainty.[10]

The problem of evil

For Christianity, the biggest problem is not belief in God as such but rather belief in God's goodness in the face of the horrendous evils we encounter in the world. The classic dilemma is that either God cannot abolish evil, in which case God is not all-powerful, or God chooses not to abolish evil, in which case God is not all-good. Many attempts have been made to meet this challenge.

Process theology argues that God is not all-powerful. The Christian Science Church argues that evil is an illusion. But to deny either the competence of God to end suffering or to question the existence of evil is to evade the issue. Traditional theology explains evil as the product of the 'fall' of the first man and the first woman. But this is too much at variance with the discoveries of archaeology, anthropology and evolutionary history to be a live option. Popular piety suggests that the problem of evil is resolved religiously in the crucifixion of Christ as God incarnate, identifying with and sharing in all our sufferings. I have never understood how the problem of evil is supposed to be helped by the notion that God also experiences it. We welcome the sympathy of friends whom we know are powerless to help us. But we would feel mocked by expressions of concern from those who have it in their power to bring relief but choose not to. The problem of evil is certainly not solved by saying that God chooses to suffer with us rather than to rescue us from our plight.

The free-will defence

Some philosophers have put forward the so-called 'free-will defence': the possibility of evil is an inescapable element of life in an objective physical world with stable laws of nature. Such a world is necessary for the emergence of free and responsible agents. If God were constantly to intervene in the world to prevent suffering then nothing we did or failed to do would matter and so we would not develop any sense of responsibility. This argument is an important one, but it cannot stand on its own as a solution to the problem of evil. For, if these free, responsible people then have their lives simply terminated by old age, disease and death, the question of why God allows evil remains unanswered.

> If people's lives are simply terminated by old age, disease and death, the question of why God allows evil remains unanswered

Why the problem of evil requires immortality

If we look at life solely from within the natural limits of human existence there is no solution to the 'problem of evil'. This world is not a hedonist's paradise. It is a struggle for existence where we earn our bread by the sweat of our brow and the endeavours of our mind. We face innumerable challenges, hardships and difficulties. Ultimately we will all age and die, unless we experience premature death through accident or disease. But the Christian perspective is not confined to this life. From its foundation Christianity has been a religion committed to belief in heaven, a divine kingdom in which sorrow and sighing have no place and in which God becomes the most central feature of our experiencing. Yet Christians have always intuited that such a world could only be appreciated and experienced by fully formed persons. We have to become 'fitted' for heaven by how we live here. Free responsible beings cannot simply be created by divine fiat. Rather, we develop characters and personalities through the way we face up to the challenges of life and thereby become persons capable of an eternal relationship with God.

The religious context of belief in a future life

This way of thinking was classically articulated by the poet John Keats. Facing terminal illness in his twenties, Keats wrote to his brother and sister, 'Do you not see how necessary a world of pain and troubles is to school an intelligence and make it a Soul . . . Call the world if you please "The Vale of Soul-making".'[11] This theme was developed most thoroughly in John Hick's greatest work, *Evil and the God of Love*. It is no part of the soul-making theodicy to say that suffering in itself is character-forming. There would be very strong evidence against so simplistic a view. But what the theodicy does say is that a real objective physical world, governed by regular physical laws, provides an environment more suited to the formation of personhood than would be provided by a paradisal environment in which divine intervention prevented all possibility of suffering.

After personhood has been fully formed, then a life of bliss in heaven becomes conceivable. But this can only be appreciated and experienced by those who have first undergone the person-forming experiences available to us in this world. Moreover, most of us will need to undergo further growth in a life after death. The soul-making theodicy is not required to suppose that the necessary growth is completed in this life. What is crucial to the theory is the claim that without belief in a future life, the Christian understanding of God as all-powerful and all-loving simply does not make sense. Life after death is essential to the coherence of theism.

Why the experience of God requires life beyond death

The essence of the Christian understanding is that God loves each one of us and that within this life we can experience real fellowship and communion with God, which God values. Jesus taught his disciples to think of God as a loving father who cherishes his prodigal children. If this is truly how God thinks of us then it

> If God loves each one of us, it becomes impossible to believe that God will allow death simply to extinguish us

becomes impossible to believe that God will allow death simply to extinguish us.

We shall see in the next chapter that the whole point of Jesus' resurrection, from the New Testament perspective, is that it is our guarantee of eternal life. The heart of Christianity would be torn out if this belief is not true.

Is belief in a divine–human relationship credible today?

In my discussion of the naturalistic case for extinction, I noted that one increasingly popular challenge to Christian belief comes from an awareness of the vastness of the universe. As Don Cupitt says, the idea that 'the Creator of a Universe sixteen billion light years across is primarily interested in the thoughts and deeds of human beings' strikes most people today as simply incongruous.[12] This overstates the case, in that it is no part of Christian doctrine that this planet is necessarily the only place in which religious experiencing should have evolved. I prefer the sentiment of Sydney Carter's hymn 'Every star shall sing a carol'. However, I accept that even assuming that only one planet in a million has evolved intelligent life, that would still leave a million million planets whose inhabitants may have evolved a religious awareness akin to our own. Is it plausible that the Creator of so vast a universe could really care about individual human beings?

It should be noted that although this challenge is now much greater than before, it is not different in kind from a tension felt from the beginning of monotheistic religion. The first unambiguously monotheistic writer in the Hebrew Bible (our Old Testament) was the Second Isaiah. For him, God was not simply the God of Israel but one whose salvation reached out to the furthest ends of the earth. Isaiah likens God's care for human beings as akin to a shepherd carrying his lambs in his bosom or as a mother caring for her sucking child. Yet Isaiah also taught that in comparison to God all the nations of the world were like a drop from a bucket, or like the fine dust on a pair of scales weighing less than nothing.[13] The idea that God relates to countless millions of human beings is mind-boggling in itself. To believe that God's loving care extends throughout the universe simply reinforces the view that for God to be as Christians believe God to be, God must be omnipotent, omniscient, omnipresent and beyond our comprehension, as well as being all-loving.

The importance of religious experience

The main ground for believing that human beings can come into a relationship with God is that they claim to do so. The Bible nowhere argues for the existence of God. Instead it tells stories about people who think they have experienced God.

> The Bible nowhere argues for the existence of God. Instead it tells stories about people who think they have experienced God

There are, for example, the stories of the call of Abraham, and of Moses feeling God speaking to him as he watches a burning bush, and there is the vision of Isaiah in the temple overcome by a sense of the holiness of God.[14] In fact, all the prophets in the Hebrew Bible talk of their call by God. In using the book of Psalms, people sing of their experiences of God and how real God is to them. The Psalter is not just the core of Jewish worship, it nourishes the spiritual life of Christian priests, monks and nuns who read from it every day. The Psalter was also the initial inspiration and model for Christian hymn-writing, in which people sing of their own religious experiences. In the New Testament we are told of the awe felt by the disciples at the presence of Christ when he called them to leave everything to follow

The religious context of belief in a future life

him. There is that mysterious account of the transfiguration of Christ, and supremely we are told that after Jesus' crucifixion his disciples had experiences that convinced them that he had triumphed over death.[15] Because of these experiences the Christian Church came into being.

Throughout Christian history, personal religious experience has inspired new creative movements. St Augustine, St Francis, St Ignatius, Luther, Wesley, to name but a few, all had dramatic conversion experiences. Christian mystics speak of their sense of the immediate presence of God, and even intellectuals like St Anselm or St Thomas Aquinas prized above all their sense of God's presence in direct mystical encounter. Schleiermacher, the 'father' of modern liberal theology, insisted that to bring Christianity back to life it was necessary to return to its source in religious experiencing. Religious experience is crucial to evangelicals. If one examines their preaching, their prayers and the hymns they sing, it becomes clear that their real grounds for faith are personal religious feelings. What matters is not an intellectual belief but the experience of being 'born again', or feeling the 'blessed assurance of salvation'.[16]

Religious experience in a global context

Experiencing transcendent reality is not solely a Christian experience. Every language-using group on this planet has a word in their vocabulary sufficiently akin to the Christian concept of God for Christian missionaries to be able to use it in communicating their own message. Language use always arises out of human experiencing. In recent years the Alister Hardy Religious Experience Research Centre has been seeking to explore religious experience as a global phenomenon. Their 'global project' was launched at a conference in London in 2004 sponsored by Modern Church. This focused on 'The God Experience'. The keynote speaker was the

The religious context of belief in a future life

Japanese Buddhist Supreme Primate, His Eminence Koken Monnyo Otani from the Tokyo Honganji. He spoke on 'Experiencing "Other Power" in Pure-land Buddhism'. His speech indicated that despite different terminologies, human experiencing can be surprisingly similar across very different religious traditions.

> Human experiencing can be surprisingly similar across very different religious traditions

The main research for the global project was done in China with assistance from scholars at seven Chinese universities, who gathered together a team of over a hundred interviewers. The research, funded by a major grant from the John Templeton Foundation, established that 56.7 per cent of Chinese claimed to have had experience of a 'mysterious spiritual "power" which they could not understand or explain clearly'.[17] At 56.7 per cent, this figure is higher than the responses in Britain to the equivalent question relating to 'a power or presence different from your everyday self', but not higher than the 65 per cent of Londoners who responded to a wider question on spirituality.[18] In parallel research to that done across mainland China, the National Chengchi University in Taiwan found that 70.8 per cent of Taiwanese claimed to have 'experience of extraordinary powers that are beyond human control'.[19] In a survey on religious experience in Turkey carried out by the University of Istanbul, 63.7 per cent of Turks reported having 'an extra-ordinary, exceptional or paranormal experience which you would classify as religious or spiritual'.[20] An Indian pilot study on religious experience in Tamil Nadu found that 68.4 per cent claimed to have had a religious experience.[21] These responses, from people in very different faith traditions and cultures, are so evidently comparable that it seems justified to claim that a common foundation in human experience lies behind the religious beliefs of human beings. It may seem incredible that millions of human beings claim awareness of a transcendent reality, but the evidence of human experience is that this is indeed the case.

The relevance of religious experience to life after death

The kind of religious experience tracked by the research described above would not in itself justify belief in immortality. But religious experience is a continuum from the relatively vague to the all-consuming. In cases where the experience is intensely personal and overwhelmingly real, a person may feel justified in believing that God would not allow them to pass into non-existence. Historically it can be shown that as Judaism shifted its emphasis from belief that God's covenant was with the people of Israel to the idea that God's New Covenant was with individual human beings, so religious thought moved in the direction of belief in life after death.[22]

Wheeler Robinson puts this well:

> The faith of the Old Testament logically points forward towards a life beyond death, because it is so sure of an inviolable fellowship with God, but . . . it does not attain to any clear vision of the goal of its journey. Nevertheless this religious faith provided the real content for the resurrection hope when this had been reached.[23]

The intensity of the religious experiencing, which became characteristic of Christianity, found expression in hymns and prayers of personal devotion proclaiming conviction in a sure and certain hope of resurrection to eternal life.

4
A historical argument for belief in the resurrection of Jesus

In his classic book *The Varieties of Religious Experience* (1902), William James argued that whatever we may think of the nature of religious experiences, they must be 'real' because they have real effects.[1] Of no experience is this more the case than in the claim of the first disciples to have seen Jesus alive after his death. This is because

> The claim of the first disciples to have seen Jesus alive after his death led to the emergence of Christianity as a dynamic new religion

the effect of those experiences was to transform the disciples' understanding, and led to the emergence of Christianity as a dynamic new religion which has subsequently become the major world faith.

The Jewish context of Jesus' teaching

A principal characteristic of contemporary New Testament scholarship is its emphasis on the Jewishness of Jesus. Dr Kathy Ehrensperger argues that current trends in historical Jesus research place the teaching of Jesus as recorded in the three synoptic Gospels fully within the ambit of liberal rabbinic thought of the first century.[2] If Jesus' life had simply ended with his crucifixion his followers might well have championed his cause for a generation or two within that tradition; but Christianity would never have developed as a separate religion. It was because of their conviction that Jesus had risen from the dead that the apostles confidently

A historical argument for belief in the resurrection of Jesus

proclaimed him as Messiah, Son of God and Saviour and set out to 'make disciples of all nations'.[3]

The proclamation of Jesus as the Messiah

The crucifixion of Jesus is one of the few facts about his life to be evidenced from hostile sources. In 110 CE the Roman historian Tacitus, in his account of Nero's persecution of 'the people called Christians', wrote that 'Christ, from whom the name was given, had been put to death in the reign of Tiberias by the procurator Pontius Pilate, and the pestilential superstition checked for a while'. But Tacitus noted that subsequently the religion had begun to 'break out afresh, not only in Judaea but also at Rome'.[4]

What this passage tells us, and what the New Testament constantly witnesses to, is that despite Jesus' ignominious death, the early Christians confidently proclaimed him as the promised 'Messiah' of Israel ('the Christ'). Indeed, this was so integral to their talk about Jesus that not only did the title Christ come to function as Jesus' surname, but his followers came to be known as 'Christians' within a generation of Jesus' death. By the time Tacitus was writing, it was simply Jesus' name. Yet the Messiahship of one whose life had been ended by public execution could never have been subsequently proclaimed to the world, if that death had really been the end.

> The Messiahship of one whose life had been ended by public execution could never have been subsequently proclaimed to the world, if that death had really been the end

The word Messiah means 'God's anointed one', and all expectations were that he would lead a successful uprising against Rome and establish God's kingdom on earth. As one of Jesus' disciples forlornly said on the road to Emmaus, 'We had been hoping that he was to be the liberator of Israel' (Luke 24.21, REB). Because Jesus' followers came to believe that he had conquered death and would

38

one day return in glory, it was possible for them to proclaim him as Messiah even more convincingly than before. But without such resurrection faith, the proclamation would have been unintelligible.

Worshipping Jesus and observance of the 'Lord's day'

The most basic Jewish belief was that God alone should be worshipped. Equally, the most characteristic Jewish practice was regular observance of the Sabbath. It is therefore of great significance that though Jesus' earliest followers were all Jews, they rapidly set aside these fundamental aspects of Judaism by their worship of Jesus, and by their observance of the first day of the week, in honour of Christ's resurrection, rather than the seventh day, in honour of God's creation of the universe. As early as St Paul's first letter to the Corinthians we learn that Christians were meeting Sunday by Sunday (1 Corinthians 16.2), while the visions in Revelation were received on 'the Lord's day' (Revelation 1.10).

In his discussion in *The Christians as the Romans Saw Them*, Robert Wilken notes that from the beginning, 'Christianity appeared to outside observers as an association devoted to the worship of Christ'.[5] Writing to the Emperor Trajan in 112 CE about what he had discovered of Christian practice, Pliny said, 'It is their habit on a fixed day to assemble and sing by turns a hymn to Christ as a god', and to bind themselves by a 'sacrament'.[6]

> It is their habit on a fixed day to assemble and sing by turns a hymn to Christ as a god and to bind themselves by a sacrament

The philosopher Celsus criticizes Christians because 'they worship to an extravagant degree this man [Jesus] who appeared recently, yet think it does not offend God if they also worship his servant.' Likewise the satirist Lucian mocks Christians for 'worshipping this man who was crucified in Palestine'.[7]

The resurrection of Jesus as the foundation of Christian hope

The religion of ancient Israel was very much focused on this life. Apart from two isolated passages (Daniel 12.1 and Isaiah 26.19), the Hebrew Bible sees this life as our one and only existence. We come from dust and will return to dust (Genesis 3.19). Talk of the spirit returning to God who gave it merely means that when we breathe out for the last time our lives come to their natural end (Ecclesiastes 12.7). This is overwhelmingly the consensus view of Old Testament scholarship.

During the inter-testamental period the possibility of a future resurrection entered Jewish thought from Zoroastrianism, and Greek ideas about the soul's immortality also became known. However, they remained speculative concepts and were firmly rejected by the Sadducees, who dominated the Jewish priesthood. For the majority of the Jewish people, it remained the case that the hope of Israel was that God would establish his kingdom on this earth, and that faithful believers would live long enough to see their children's children and peace in Israel (Psalm 128.6).

In contrast to all this, Christianity burst upon the world with an absolute conviction about life after death. As the author of 1 Peter puts it: 'Blessed be the God and Father of our Lord Jesus Christ! By his great mercy we have been born anew to a living hope through the Resurrection of Jesus Christ from the dead, and to an inheritance which is imperishable, undefiled and unfading, kept in heaven for you' (1 Peter 1.3–4, RSV). Every book of the New Testament was written from that perspective. As a matter of history there is no doubt at all that the resurrection of Jesus gave rise to a wholly new confidence in a life beyond.

> As a matter of history there is no doubt at all that the resurrection of Jesus gave rise to a wholly new confidence in a life beyond

A historical argument for belief in the resurrection of Jesus

Adolf Harnack summed up the position thus, in his 1901 book *What is Christianity?*

> Whatever may have happened at the grave and in the manner of the appearances, one thing is certain: This grave was the birthplace of the indestructible belief that death is vanquished, that there is life eternal. It is useless to cite Plato; it is useless to point to the Persian religion, and the ideas and the literature of later Judaism. All this would have perished and has perished; but the certainty of the resurrection and of a life eternal which is bound up with the grave in Joseph's garden has not perished, and on the conviction that 'Jesus lives' we still base those hopes of citizenship in an Eternal City which makes our earthly life worth living.[8]

The Easter faith of the early Church

One thing that both Christian and pagan writers agree on is that the early Christians were so completely confident in the future hope that they willingly embraced death, and in so doing they gradually converted the Roman world. According to St Athanasius, 'the best evidence for the resurrection of Jesus' is the way that Christians 'treat death as nothing . . . they go eagerly to meet it . . . rather than remain in this present life'.[9] This argument could only be persuasive if it were in fact true that Christians really did treat death as nothing. Historical evidence for such faith comes from their enthusiasm for martyrdom. Emperor Trajan, while recognizing that failure to participate in the imperial rites was a capital offence, had nonetheless ordered that Christians were 'not to be sought out', nor should anonymous tip-offs be followed up.[10] But Trajan's policy of turning a blind eye was wrecked by Christians openly declaring themselves to be Christians and handing themselves in to the authorities for execution. Studies of the early martyrologies shows that at least two-thirds of the martyrs were 'volunteers' in this way.[11]

A historical argument for belief in the resurrection of Jesus

Roman writers were well aware of the strength with which Christians held such views. The physician Galen found hope for life after death quite baffling in the light of his physiological knowledge, while the satirist Lucian said of Christians, 'The poor wretches have convinced themselves that they are going to be immortal and live for all time.'[12]

A summary of the historical case

The historical case for believing in the resurrection of Jesus is that the Easter faith of the first Jewish disciples of Jesus requires some sufficient explanation. As we have seen, it seems historically certain that they proclaimed Jesus as the Messiah, that they worshipped him, that they substituted the day of his resurrection for the Jewish Sabbath and they were so convinced that Jesus had conquered death that they persuaded others to share this extraordinary belief and were themselves prepared to die as witnesses to it. If Jesus had in fact appeared to them in some sufficiently convincing manner, then all these developments are explicable. Without it, the birth of Christianity as a world religion becomes a complete mystery.

> Without Jesus' resurrection, the birth of Christianity as a world religion becomes a complete mystery

The earliest tradition

The earliest tradition relating to the resurrection of Jesus is that recorded by St Paul. He tells the Corinthians, 'I handed on to you what I myself received' (1 Corinthians 15.3). What he handed on did not include any account of Jesus' tomb being found empty but was solely a record of Jesus' appearances to his disciples, ending with the appearance to St Paul himself. In speaking of these appearances Paul always uses the deponent verb *opthe*, which Professor

A historical argument for belief in the resurrection of Jesus

C. F. Evans argues 'cannot be translated "he was seen by" but means "he let himself be seen"'.[13] It is a word more commonly used for a religious vision than for something physically seen. This suggests that for St Paul the appearances should be understood as inward events. 'God revealed his son within me' is how he describes his own experience in Galatians 1.15. In Acts 26.19 he calls it 'a heavenly vision'. St Paul's statement that 'flesh and blood can never possess the kingdom of God' (1 Corinthians 15.50, REB) suggests that he did not suppose that Jesus' flesh and blood had done so. Likewise, St Paul's wish that he could leave his home in the body in order to be with the Lord (2 Corinthians 5.6–9) implies a conviction that Jesus had also left his earthly body behind.

The surprising endings of the Gospels of St Mark and St Matthew

All the most ancient manuscripts of St Mark's Gospel end at chapter 16 verse 8. Later manuscripts add a variety of alternative endings, indirectly confirming that what St Mark originally wrote ended at verse 8. What we have at the end of St Mark is an account of the women finding the tomb of Jesus empty, followed by an explanation that the reason the women said nothing about this to anyone was that they were afraid. If the empty tomb had been part of the earliest tradition, there would have been no need to say that the women were silent and explain that silence. This is why St Mark had to justify (either his own, or his sources') adding an empty tomb story.

The ending of St Matthew's Gospel is also significant. It records an account of an appearance of Jesus in which he gave 'the great commission' to 'make all nations his disciples'. We are told that when the disciples saw Jesus 'they worshipped him; but some doubted' (Matthew 28.17, RSV). Both reactions suggest that what some of the disciples experienced was a heavenly vision such as

St Paul had talked of. Those who experienced the vision worshipped, while others doubted the reality of the experience. If the appearance had been a straightforward seeing, such as a camera might have recorded, there would have been no grounds for either the worship or the doubt.

The empty tomb tradition

It is, of course, possible that St Mark's explanation for the women's silence was correct and that the subsequent circulation of accounts of the empty tomb provided helpful support for belief in the resurrection of Jesus. The empty tomb stories are recorded in all four Gospels and their format takes the common pattern of 'pronouncement stories', which in the opinion of form critics are 'the type of narrative likely to have the greatest historical reliability'.[14] The majority of Christians are very reluctant to reject these accounts, and so they integrate them with the resurrection appearances by saying that Jesus' dead body was physically transformed into a new 'spiritual body' subject to quite different physical laws.

The case for a spiritual body

There is no New Testament support for a bodily resurrection understood as the resuscitation of Jesus' corpse.

> There is no New Testament support for a bodily resurrection understood as the resuscitation of Jesus' corpse

Jesus did not rise from the dead like Lazarus or Jairus' daughter, only to die again later. Jesus' disciples believed that he had conquered death. Consequently, if the empty tomb is believed to be an essential part of the resurrection story then the reason the tomb was empty was that Jesus' mortal body had put on immortality. This may be the position presented in 1 Peter 3.18, which speaks of Jesus being 'put to death in the flesh but made alive in the spirit', and it alone would make sense of the sustained contrast between earthly bodies and heavenly bodies throughout 1 Corinthians 15.35–56. It is true that there are passages in Luke and John that speak of Jesus' risen body in more corporeal terms. In Luke 24 Jesus invites his disciples to touch him, to see that he has flesh and bones as they have, and he eats and drinks with them to make the same point. Yet the very same chapter talks of Jesus suddenly 'vanishing from their sight', or equally suddenly 'appearing in their midst' or suddenly 'parting from them', and in some manuscript traditions being 'carried up into heaven' (Luke 24.51, RSV). John likewise has Jesus inviting the disciples to touch him, yet on both occasions when Jesus makes this invitation he is said to have appeared suddenly in the middle of a locked room (John 20.19, 26). A body that can appear and vanish at will is so utterly unlike an earthly body that it is difficult to understand what is gained by claiming material continuity between the two. In practice, it is hard to see any significant difference between a 'spiritual body' capable of materializing and dematerializing at will and a wholly visionary appearance of Jesus.

Why diversity of views about the nature of Jesus resurrection is inevitable

In the early years of the twentieth century the Church of England was engulfed by controversies about the resurrection of Jesus. Partly in response to these a Commission on Doctrine in the Church of England was established. In 1938 it affirmed unanimously that the belief that Jesus had risen from the dead was 'an essential part of the Christian message'. However, it also affirmed that belief in the truth of the resurrection is compatible with 'a variety of critical views' about what had actually happened. Most of the commissioners were content to affirm the 'traditional explanation that the tomb was empty', but they recognized that 'others of us

A historical argument for belief in the resurrection of Jesus

would maintain... that the general freedom long claimed and used in the interpretation of the clause "the resurrection of the flesh" cannot leave the interpretation of the other clause, "the third day he rose again from the dead", unaffected'. They concluded that in view of the 'complications of the discussion... it was not surprising that opinions should differ... on how much in the record is... derived from... fact and how much is due... to interpretation'. They also felt that however good the historical record was thought to be, 'there would still be room for difference of judgement on how much was seen with the bodily eye and how much with spiritual vision'.[15]

> However good the historical record, there would still be room for difference of judgement on how much was seen with the bodily eye and how much with spiritual vision

Modernist interpretations of the resurrection

Throughout the twentieth century 'modernists' (as members of Modern Church have come to be known) characteristically argued for a spiritual interpretation of Jesus' resurrection.[16] St Paul regarded it as axiomatic that the resurrection of Jesus was the primary ground for supposing that we too might live beyond the grave (1 Corinthians 15.12–19). The modernists felt that they would be false to St Paul's most basic belief if they interpreted the resurrection of Jesus in such a way as to make it radically different from what will happen to us. Our bodies will disintegrate. If Jesus' corpse was changed directly into a spiritual body, it would be less relevant to our own future hopes. By contrast, if the resurrection appearances of Jesus were religious visions which convinced the disciples of his personal immortality, they would give us grounds for hoping that we too might share this destiny.

5
The evidential and religious value of near-death experiences

What are near-death experiences?

In recent years modern medicine has been able to resuscitate people from the brink of death. About 10 per cent of the people brought back from death have memories of what they think happened to them while they were apparently dead. These reports are controversial. We should not speak of people having died – we only hear their stories because they did not die. Hence it is usual to talk of near-death experiences (NDEs). What is certain is that these experiences happened to people whose hearts had stopped beating and whose lungs had stopped breathing. Research by Dr Sam Parnia and Dr Peter Fenwick at Southampton hospital shows that after a few seconds there was also no measurable brain activity.

> These experiences happened to people whose hearts had stopped beating and whose lungs had stopped breathing

What people describe

People who report an NDE say that they found themselves outside their bodies watching the resuscitation attempts. Many relate other experiences, such as being met by deceased relatives and friends or by a 'being of light' who seems full of love and understanding. Some report reviewing their past lives; 82 per cent experience a sense of calmness and peace, 40 per cent a sense of joy and 38 per cent a sense of love; 72 per cent report that their lives were changed by the experience and 82 per cent say that they no longer have any fear of death. Most believe that if they had not been brought back, they would have gone on to a new life.[1]

One per cent have frightening negative experiences, but it is interesting to note that these hellish images fade and the people concerned see them as far less significant than other kinds of experience, and as a stage in a journey towards a light beyond them.[2]

Naturalistic explanations

What causes these experiences to happen? Most doctors say that they are caused by physiological changes in the brain.

> Most doctors say that NDEs are caused by physiological changes in the brain

Such brain-state phenomena are described in great detail by Professor Michael Marsh in *Out-of-Body and Near-Death Experiences.*[3] Naturalistic explanations can make sense of many features of near-death experiences. For example, if a person's heart has stopped beating then blood will no longer be oxygenating the brain, and shortage of oxygen can bring about hallucinations of a religious kind. Reduced blood pressure in the middle ear would make people feel that they were floating in space. Most terminally ill people will be on powerful pain-killing drugs like morphine or ketamine. They will also be suffering psychological stress.

Some problems with naturalistic explanations

However, there are problems with naturalistic explanations. If the experiences were simply caused by oxygen starvation, one would expect other people who suffer from shortage of oxygen, like test-pilots or Himalayan mountaineers, to have the same kind of experiences. But they don't. Hallucinations caused by oxygen starvation or drugs are confused, incoherent and swiftly forgotten, whereas NDEs have great clarity and often lead to a change of life. Moreover, a survey of 2,000 hospital staff concerning the medical condition of their dying patients found that in fact there was no correlation at all between their having an NDE and factors such as oxygen starvation, drug regime, or type of psychological state.[4]

> A hospital survey concerning the medical condition of dying patients found no correlation between having an NDE and oxygen starvation, drug regime, or psychological state

The observations made during 'out-of-the-body' states

The most striking feature of the NDE is that very often people experience looking down from above on their unconscious bodies. One example of such cases is what happened to Dr Gordon McPhate, now Dean of Chester Cathedral but for most of his career director of medical teaching and senior lecturer in pathology at St Andrews University Medical School. When Dr McPhate was 18 and already committed to a medical career he was involved in a car crash in which he almost died. While the paramedics were trying to release him from the wreckage, his heart stopped beating and he found himself out of his body looking on at what was happening. This changed his life completely. Thinking back on this experience from his later position as a medical pathologist, Dr McPhate says that 'science alone could not make sense of my being outside my body, watching myself being resuscitated by paramedics'. As well as observing the event Dr McPhate had a profound religious experience while outside his body, which changed his life. This involved seeing a being of radiant light who seemed so loving that he had no wish to return to this world.

The evidential and religious value of near-death experiences

However, 'somehow it was communicated that I was to come back for a purpose'. At the time of this event Dr McPhate was not a Christian, but finding a Bible by his bed in hospital he read the beginning of John's Gospel and concluded that he must have encountered 'the light which enlightens everyone who comes into the world'.[5]

> He encountered 'the light which enlightens everyone who comes into the world'

My own out-of-the-body experience

Thinking over Dr McPhate's description of what happened to him at 18 has made me think over the possible significance of something that happened to me at the age of 16. I was on a cycling holiday with a group of friends in the Brecon Beacons. One day we were deluged in a thunderstorm and I remember pushing my bike up a hill, soaked to the skin and utterly exhausted, when suddenly the thunder and lightning seemed to come simultaneously and I found myself lying on the ground. Or more correctly, I found myself up in the air looking down on my unconscious body. It only lasted an instant before I was back in my body and getting up again. I don't know what happened. I couldn't have been near death, otherwise I wouldn't have been able to get up, and then walk and cycle a further six miles after the event. But I remember to this day looking down on my body. What I also remember is that shortly after the event I wrote a poem about it. What strikes me now as interesting is that instead of describing myself as going out of my body I used the phrase 'now that I have been with God'. I do wonder whether one reason why belief in both the soul and God have always seemed self-evident to me, but not to most of my contemporaries, is that

> For a couple of seconds, I found myself outside my body and conscious of the presence of God

for a couple of seconds, when I was 16, I found myself outside my body and conscious of the presence of God.

The case of Pam Reynolds

Dr Michael Sabom found an interesting case involving a patient, Pam Reynolds, who underwent a life-threatening operation to remove an aneurysm from her brain. To prevent blood circulating around her head during the operation her heart was stopped, her body temperature was lowered, and she was for all practical purposes temporarily dead with no measurable brain function. Nevertheless, after the operation she described much of what happened during it.

> She told the doctors that the drill that opened up her skull vibrated at a natural D

She was a professional musician and told the doctors that the drill that opened up her skull vibrated at a natural D.

None of the doctors had a clue about the musical note at which the drill vibrated. But they found that she was right.[6] This case is controversial. Michael Marsh points to some inaccuracies in her account. On the other hand, in the BBC documentary *The Day I Died* the doctors actually involved relate that they were struck by how much she got right.[7]

The significance of out-of-the-body observations

A recent handbook for clinicians, covering the past 35 years of research into NDEs, defines them as occurring when a person near the point of death experiences their consciousness as separated from the body.[8] The phenomenon of going 'out of the body' at the time of apparent death and 'looking down from above' on the resuscitation attempts is the most evidential aspect of the near-death experience for belief in the soul.

The evidential and religious value of near-death experiences

For doctors who have researched in this field, it is the experiences of their patients that have first convinced them of the importance of NDEs. In 1982, in one of the first television documentaries on NDEs, Dr Peter Fenwick was included as a medical expert in order to explain which parts of the brain were responsible for these strange hallucinations.[9] However, he subsequently followed up NDE accounts from his patients, and these convinced him that their experiences could not be explained away in this manner as purely physiological. He went on to collect and analyse 344 British cases and became the leading advocate for NDE research.

> The phenomenon of going 'out of the body' at the time of apparent death and 'looking down from above' is the most evidential aspect of the NDE for belief in the soul

Even the most resolutely sceptical researcher into NDEs, Dr Susan Blackmore, accepts that 'there is no doubt that people describe reasonably accurately events that have occurred around them during their NDE'. She seeks to explain them naturalistically as a combination of 'prior knowledge, fantasy, and lucky guesses' and the remaining operating senses of hearing and touch'.[10] People who have actually had these experiences, however, find such explanations unsatisfactory. The large number of correct observations that do not fit into any of Blackmore's explanatory categories (other than the catch-all category of 'lucky guesses') suggests that the data cannot be accounted for by such explanations.

Blackmore's hypothesis has been tested by Dr Penny Sartori, who worked as a staff nurse in an intensive therapy unit. She asked a control group of patients consisting of people who had been resuscitated without having the distinctive NDE experience if they could describe what happened to them in the resuscitation process. Almost all of them made major errors in describing the resuscitation procedures. This contrasted strongly with those who had reported having a classic NDE, whose accounts were substantially correct.[11]

NDEs in non-Christian religious traditions

Belief in the immortality of the soul is common to many religions. In his book *Conceptions of the Afterlife in Early Civilizations*, Dr Gregory Shushan shows that in widely separated cultures (Ancient Egypt and Mesopotamia, Vedic India, pre-Buddhist China, and pre-conquest Meso-America) some commonalities in afterlife beliefs suggest experience of NDEs.[12]

> Belief in the immortality of the soul is common to many religions

Early Israelite religion is unusual in that it had no real concept of the soul, yet in subsequent Jewish thought belief in the soul's immortality became central. In a Jewish mystical text called the *Zohar* we read: 'We have learned that at the hour of a man's departure from the world, his father and relatives gather round him and he sees and recognises them . . . and they accompany his soul to the place where it is to abide.'[13]

Tibetan religion makes similar claims. In *The Tibetan Book of the Dead* we read that when a person's 'consciousness-principle' gets outside the body, 'He sees his relatives and friends gathered round weeping and watches as they remove the clothes from the body or take away the bed.'[14] NDEs have long been acknowledged as religiously significant in Tibet, in that 'returnees from death' (*deloks*) have for centuries been regarded as important witnesses concerning the reality of the next world.[15]

In Greek philosophy Plato was the best-known advocate of the immortality of the soul. One source of his confidence may have been a story he had been told of a soldier called Er who was thought to have been killed but just before his cremation had 'come back to life and told the story of what he had seen in the other world'.[16]

In Islam it is clear that a strong ecstatic element was present in all Muhammad's revelatory experiences. In one of his collected sayings (*hadith*) he said: 'Never once did I have a revelation without feeling that my soul was being torn away from me.'[17] His 'night journey', in which he ascended through the seven heavens, has been interpreted by some in the Sufi tradition as an 'annihilation' (*fana*) followed by 'revival' (*baqa*), in which Muhammad passed through death to the vision of God and was restored to life with a greatly enhanced spirituality.[18]

> Muhammad passed through death to the vision of God and was restored to life with a greatly enhanced spirituality

NDEs and Christianity

Within Christianity the peak of mystical experience has always been described in terms of 'ecstasy', which literally means 'out of the body'. When St Paul found his religious authority challenged by the Corinthians he rested his claim to their respect explicitly on an experience that reads very much like a contemporary NDE.

> I know a Christian man who fourteen years ago (whether in the body or out of the body, I do not know – God knows) was caught up as far as the third heaven. And I know that this same man (whether in the body or apart from the body, I do not know – God knows) was caught up into paradise, and heard words so secret that human lips may not repeat them. About such a man I am ready to boast.[19]

St Paul was speaking autobiographically here, as a few verses later he laments that 'to keep me from being unduly elated by the magnificence of such revelations I was given a thorn in the flesh'.[20] St Paul's experience included out-of-the-body experiences and visions of paradise, both of which are key features of the near-death experience.

> St Paul's experience included out-of-the-body experiences and visions of paradise

Commenting on these verses, St John of the Cross, the great sixteenth-century mystic, remarked that such experiences normally only occur when the soul 'goes forth from the flesh and departs this mortal life'. But St Paul was allowed these visions by special grace. Such visions, however, occur 'very rarely and to very few'.[21] St John of the Cross almost certainly had an NDE himself, for his poems talk of 'living without inhabiting myself', 'dying yet I do not die', and 'soaring to the heavens'.[22]

Experiences of a 'being of light'

One feature of NDEs is that 72 per cent of contemporary near-death experiencers report seeing a radiant light, which they often describe as a loving presence and sometimes name in accordance with a religious figure from their own traditions. *The Tibetan Book of the Dead* speaks of the dying person seeing the radiant, pure and immutable light of Amida Buddha before passing into what is explicitly described as a world of mental images. Catholic tradition, for example in Cardinal Newman's *Dream of Gerontius*, has spoken of how angels of light will receive us at death. Heavenly visions have always associated God with radiant light, and traditionally saints are painted surrounded by a halo of light. Likewise 'seeing the light' has long been a metaphor for religious conversion.

The 'being of light' described by contemporary experiencers is always named in accordance with the religious tradition of the percipient. According to *The Tibetan Book of the Dead*, 'The *Dharmakaya* (deity) of clear light will appear in whatever shape will benefit all beings.' Commenting on this verse for his English translation, Lama Kazi Dawa-Samdup says:

The evidential and religious value of near-death experiences

> To appeal to a Shivaite devotee, the form of Shiva is assumed; to a Buddhist the form of the Buddha ... to a Christian, the form of Jesus; to a Muslim the form of the Prophet; and so for other religious devotees; and for all manner and conditions of mankind a form appropriate to the occasion.[23]

This seems a good way of making sense of the fact that people of a wide range of traditions have similar experiences of a 'being of light', but they each name it in accordance with their own religious background.

This is even true of atheists. When the prominent twentieth-century atheist philosopher A. J. Ayer had an NDE, he said afterwards, 'I realised the light was responsible for the government of the universe', and also that 'on the face of it this experience is rather strong evidence for life after death'. Later he retracted his claim, saying that it had 'only slightly weakened' his belief that death would be the end but he continued to hope it would be. Finally he retracted even that.[24]

Many resuscitated people claim that this 'being of light' knows them completely and has limitless compassion to them in welcoming them into the life beyond. It is interesting that this is remarkably like what the Pure-land scriptures say: 'The Buddha of Infinite Light and Boundless Life' (*Amida*) has vowed to appear at the moment of death. Consequently, when people 'come to the end of life they will be met by Amida Buddha and the Bodhisattvas of Compassion and Wisdom and will be led by them into Buddha's Land'.[25] This combination of radiant light, wisdom and compassion correspond precisely to the descriptions given by the resuscitated of their experience of this encounter.

In recent years the idea that anything at all could continue after death has been rejected by many because such a notion is so much at variance with our normative materialist understanding of reality. It is fascinating, therefore, that now, as a result of modern medicine's ability to resuscitate people who have apparently 'died', we appear to be gathering information that is suggestive that historic beliefs in a real life beyond may have some evidential support.

Proof of heaven?

This possibility has been greatly enhanced by the publication in 2012 of Eben Alexander's *Proof of Heaven: A Neurosurgeon's Journey into the Afterlife*.[26] During a lifetime of brain research, including 15 years as a professor of neurosurgery at Harvard, Dr Alexander authored or co-authored more than 1,500 academic articles on the brain, but he had never taken NDEs seriously until he had one himself. His was an unusual case in that he was on the brink of death not just for a few minutes but for a whole week. Yet while totally comatose he had a succession of transcendent experiences that convinced him of the absolute reality of God, the soul and the future life. After his recovery he was able to examine his medical records and discuss them with his fellow neurosurgeons. It was clear that the areas of his brain responsible for thought and feeling had completely closed down during his coma, and yet inexplicably he had had the most profoundly real experiences of his life during this time. For him, this was indeed 'proof of heaven'.

For those who have not had such an experience, what happened to Dr Alexander cannot provide 'proof'. Yet when combined with the accounts of thousands of other people from a wide variety of religious traditions and from across the centuries, NDEs do need to be taken seriously. They strongly suggest that the dominant naturalistic understanding of reality may not be the whole truth and that human destiny may indeed not be limited to the horizons of our present existence.

6

Moral and religious arguments against belief in hell

The location of the traditional hell

Traditional doctrine teaches that there will be one definitive last judgement in which the whole of humankind will be separated into two groups: the saved will receive God's blessing and enter eternal life, the damned will receive his curse and be thrown into a lake of fire and brimstone with the devil and his angels, there to be tortured day and night for ever.[1]

Volcanoes were surely the source of belief in a lake of fire beneath the earth. Early Christian writers, including St Augustine, noted that if one looked down into the craters of Etna and Vesuvius one would see that the fire and brimstone within those 'vent-holes of hell' appeared to burn continuously without being consumed.[2] On this basis it seemed reasonable to suppose that the lake of fire beneath the earth would always burn, but never consume, the bodies of the damned.[3] The Fathers' observations were, of course, faulty and the whole idea of a fiery underworld as a suitable location for the endless punishment of wicked human beings is unthinkable today.

> The whole idea of a fiery underworld as a suitable location for the endless punishment of wicked human beings is unthinkable today

Torment as spectacle

In Revelation 14.10–11 we are told that the damned will be 'tormented in sulphurous flames in the presence of the holy angels

Moral and religious arguments against belief in hell

and the Lamb' (REB). This verse led to one of the worst aberrations within Christian theology, namely the belief that one of the greatest joys of the saints in heaven would be derived from watching the sufferings of the damned. Tertullian gloatingly wrote:

> At that greatest of all spectacles, how shall I admire, how laugh, how rejoice when I behold ... so many magistrates liquefying in fiercer flames than they ever kindled against the Christians; so many sage philosophers blushing in red-hot fires with their deluded pupils ... so many dancers tripping more nimbly from anguish than ever before from applause.[4]

In the twelfth century similar sentiments found expression in *The Sentences* of Peter Lombard: 'The elect shall go forth ... to see the sufferings of the impious and seeing this they will not be affected by grief but will be satiated with joy at the sight of the unutterable calamity of the impious.'[5] Lombard's *Sentences* was the standard textbook of Catholic theology during the Middle Ages; it was not replaced by the *Summa Theologiae* of St Thomas Aquinas (1225–74) until the sixteenth century. But Aquinas took a similar position on hell as a spectacle, stating that: 'In order that the happiness of the saints may be more delightful to them and that they may give more copious thanks to God for it, a perfect view of the sufferings of the damned is granted to them.'[6]

The Council of Florence and the Spanish Inquisition

Historically the first declaration that the Church was to adopt and explicitly teach a wholly exclusive understanding of salvation was made at the Council of Florence of 1438–45. It was stated:

> No one remaining outside the Church, not just pagans, but also Jews or heretics or schismatics, can become partakers of eternal life; but they will go to the everlasting fire prepared for the devil and his angels unless before the end of life they are joined to the Church.[7]

Moral and religious arguments against belief in hell

The papal theological adviser at this Council was Cardinal Jean de Torquemada. It was no accident that his nephew, Tomas de Torquemada, became the Grand Inquisitor of Spain. If one seriously believes that all non-Christians will be tortured for ever in hell then it really does become an act of charity to use all possible means to bring about their conversion. The uncle's theology foreshadowed the nephew's practice. In England, Queen Mary justified her persecution on religious grounds: 'As the souls of heretics are hereafter to be eternally burning in hell, there can be nothing more proper than for me to imitate the Divine vengeance by burning them on earth.'[8]

The multiple tortures of hell

At the time of the Counter-Reformation the teaching about hell became even more virulent. According to the Catechism of the Council of Trent (1545–63), the torments of hell consisted not merely in burning but would comprise 'an accumulation of all punishments'.[9] Such views were not confined to Catholic thinkers. To read the lurid descriptions in 'hell-fire' sermons preached by evangelical clergy over the centuries is to realize the depths of sadistic imagination to which the human spirit can sink when people believe that they have divine authority for such thoughts.[10] There is abundant evidence to support Don Cupitt's claim that 'Christians became cruel men, because they believed in a cruel God.'[11] Certainly the inquisitors' manuals of torture exactly mirrored what they believed God had in store for heretics. Likewise Ian Bradley has found that in the Victorian period, the worst cases of cruelty to children happened in evangelical homes where there was a preoccupation with belief in hell.[12]

> In the Victorian period, the worst cases of cruelty to children happened in evangelical homes where there was a preoccupation with belief in hell

The moral case against hell[13]

In 1830 F. D. E. Schleiermacher argued that the existence of hell would make heaven impossible. The more truly Christ-like a person became, the more concerned one would be for the suffering of others. Consequently, no truly saintly person could be perfectly happy in heaven while aware that others were suffering in hell.[14] This argument represents a major moral advance, turning on its head the earlier idea that one of the greatest joys of heaven would be to watch the damned being tortured.[15]

The moral case against hell was taken further by F. D. Maurice, who argued in 1853 that belief in hell was in direct contradiction to the primal and quite decisive Christian doctrine of the love of God: 'If we start from belief that "God is actually love"', we shall 'dread any representation of Him which is at variance with this [and] will shrink from attributing to Him acts which would be unlovely in man'.[16]

> Belief in hell is in direct contradiction to the primal and quite decisive Christian doctrine of the love of God

Maurice believed that the doctrine of hell made a mockery of Jesus' picture of the loving fatherhood of God. For if it were indeed the case that all humanity is damned except those who accept Christ as their personal saviour, it would condemn 'most of the American slaves, and the whole body of Turks, Hindus, Hottentots and Jews ... to hopeless destruction'. Such a conclusion 'would negate belief in the infinite love of our heavenly Father and utterly destroy the credibility of the Christian gospel'.[17]

'Hell dismissed with costs'

H. B. Wilson, in an essay published in 1860, challenged belief in hell on the grounds that people do not come in two clear-cut categories.[18] He felt that no one at the time of death is so utterly good or so

Moral and religious arguments against belief in hell

spiritually mature either to deserve or to fully appreciate instant translation to eternal bliss in intimate communication and fellowship with God. Equally, no one is so wholly evil as to merit nothing but endless torture. Wilson felt, therefore, that there must be room for development after death in an intermediate state. He was prosecuted for heresy for denying hell, but at the trial was completely cleared by the Judicial Committee of the Privy Council. This legal case led to the celebrated headline 'Hell dismissed with costs'. A key factor in his acquittal was that in the sixteenth century, Forty-Two Articles of Religion had been drafted as the doctrinal foundation for the Church of England. But some were removed before the final version, the Thirty-Nine Articles, was promulgated in the Elizabethan settlement of 1571. One of the articles dropped had affirmed belief in everlasting torment. The Lord Chancellor, on behalf of the Judicial Committee of the Privy Council, ruled that this omission meant that, since the Elizabethan settlement, the Church of England has never required its clergy to believe in hell, even if at that time the vast majority of its clergy did so.

> Since the Elizabethan settlement, the Church of England has never required its clergy to believe in hell

Wilson's acquittal was important for F. D. Maurice, who had lost his chair at King's College, London for his earlier denial of hell; he was now rehabilitated and appointed to a chair at Cambridge. The two Archbishops issued a dissenting note, accepting the correctness of the judicial verdict but affirming that in their view Anglicans ought to believe in hell. Shortly afterwards, approximately half the clergy signed a petition to say that they did believe in everlasting torment, but it is notable that almost all the leading thinkers of the Church refused to sign. Since that time, belief in hell has gone into steep decline. Wilson's alternative of an intermediate state has been seen as a more Christian alternative, and this has sometimes been related to the Roman Catholic doctrine of purgatory. Belief both in an intermediate state and in purgatory allows for the possibility of development after death so as to become 'fitted for heaven'.

A backlash in defence of hell

Although belief in hell has faded from the consciousness of many, this is by no means universal. In 1981 the University and Colleges Christian Fellowship, which formerly had made no explicit mention of hell, introduced an affirmation concerning hell into its doctrinal basis. Since 1995 all officers of university Christian Unions are required to affirm belief that 'the Lord Jesus will return in person, to judge everyone, to execute God's just condemnation on those who have not repented and to receive the redeemed into eternal glory'. In 2000 a report of the Evangelical Alliance reaffirmed belief in hell: 'As well as separation from God, hell involves severe punishment ... both physical and psychological', and will be 'conscious experience of rejection and torment'.[19] The primary reason for this is their belief that the doctrine of hell was taught by Jesus himself and hence must remain an inescapable part of the Christian message, however much this may dismay their consciences.

The evangelical dilemma

Many evangelicals are acutely conscious that by all normal standards, hell is a doctrine of appalling cruelty.

For example, J. A. Motyer, a former principal of one of the leading Anglican evangelical college, writes:

> the idea of eternal ruin ... simply cannot be allowed to continue as a possibility if there is any allowable way of escaping from it. Every sensitive spirit will shrink from ... the

Many evangelicals are acutely conscious that by all normal standards, hell is a doctrine of appalling cruelty

horror involved in taking the New Testament threats of endless anguish in what appears at first sight to be their plain meaning.

However, Motyer believes that 'the facts, in so far as they are revealed', allow no escape from the doctrine. If Holy Scripture teaches everlasting punishment then 'we can only seek humbly to follow what is written for our learning'. This is in spite of the fact that on Motyer's own admission such teaching offends our reason, love, sympathy and sensitivity. But 'God is greater than ... our finite logic', and 'His ways are not our ways, nor our thoughts his thoughts.'[20]

One can feel only sympathy for a man who imprisoned himself inside a system of thought that horrified his conscience. But there are two ways by which evangelicals could leave this Bastille. First, the doctrine of revelation itself requires belief that the language God uses to reveal himself should be adequate to its purpose. Consequently, if God centrally reveals himself as self-giving love, it would be contrary to that central message to attribute unlovely actions to him. The quotation Motyer alludes to comes from Isaiah, and continues: 'for my ways are *higher* than your ways and my thoughts than your thoughts'.[21] If a doctrine offends our highest moral feelings, that is a powerful reason for rejecting it. Indeed, the Victorian rejection of belief in hell was precisely on this basis. As J. S. Mill declared, 'I will call no being "good" who is not what I mean when I apply that epithet to my fellow creatures; and if such a being can sentence me to hell for not so calling him, to hell I will go.'[22]

The heart of Jesus' message

The second issue is the interpretation of the New Testament. It is unfortunate that Motyer felt content with what seemed 'at first sight' to be the 'plain meaning' of Scripture. The consensus of New Testament scholarship, which seeks by critical study to set Jesus'

Moral and religious arguments against belief in hell

teaching in the context of first-century religious thought, is that although Jesus freely used the imagery of eternal judgement, it does not appear to have been in any way central to his own thought.

The two parables most often cited as evidence that Jesus believed in hell are those of Dives and Lazarus, and of the sheep and the goats. However, the message that Jesus used these stories to drive home was that it is contrary to God's will for the fortunate in this life to live in pleasure, completely indifferent to the sufferings of the poor and needy. Since Jesus taught his disciples to pray that God's will should be done on earth *as it is in heaven*, it is inconceivable to suppose that what he wanted to teach was that the divisions between human beings that he found so intolerable on earth would be intensified and continued for ever in the next world, albeit with a reversal of positions! One of the perils facing a teacher who uses popular imagery to illustrate a point is that all too often his hearers remember the image rather than the message. This seems to have happened to Jesus in these parables.

> Although Jesus freely used the imagery of eternal judgement, it does not appear to have been in any way central to his own thought

> It is inconceivable that Jesus wanted to teach that the divisions between human beings on earth would be intensified and continued for ever in the next world

New Testament scholars agree that Jesus' teaching about the loving fatherhood of God was the most distinctive and characteristic aspect of his thought. 'Father' as a title of God was extremely rare in rabbinic Judaism, but it was the way Jesus almost invariably spoke of God. The cry of dereliction from the cross was the only time that Jesus did not address God as Father. The parable of the prodigal son likens God to a father who is always ready to accept and forgive. It is a useful exercise to go through the Gospels and examine all the occasions at which Jesus was in controversy with the scribes and the Pharisees. It readily becomes apparent that the biggest difference was that they disagreed with Jesus' teaching about the need to exhibit unlimited forgiveness to sinners. In the light of these considerations, it is strange indeed to suppose that a message of everlasting torture was ever associated with Jesus' name. Loving fathers do not torture their children. Still less would they wish to torture them day and night for ever. From the perspectives of belief in the forgiveness of sins and belief in natural justice, the idea of endless punishment could never be justified.

Hell in the mainstream of Anglican and Catholic thought today

Within the Church of England, the doctrine of hell was finally repudiated as incompatible with belief in the love of God by the Doctrine Commission of 1996, in their report *The Mystery of Salvation*. Mainstream Roman Catholic teaching has also, I think, rejected belief in everlasting torment. Preaching in the Vatican shortly before his election in 1978, Pope John Paul II suggested:

> in the light of the truth that 'God is Love' we should countenance tentatively reaching out towards some later phase in the history of salvation – not disclosed in revelation and the scriptures – which might put an end to this separation between those who are saved and those who are damned.[23]

> Every human being without any exception whatever has been redeemed by Christ

Following his election to the papacy he was less tentative and in his first and greatest encyclical letter, *Redemptor Hominis*, he affirmed this: 'Every human being without any exception whatever has been redeemed by Christ because Christ is in a way united to the human person – every person without exception even if the individual may not realize this fact.'[24]

Moral and religious arguments against belief in hell

However, the Roman Catholic Church finds it particularly hard to repudiate explicitly ideas that were once widely accepted. Consequently, sporadic references to hell are still made by Church leaders, including, notably, Pope Benedict XVI: on 27 March 2007 he was reported as teaching that 'the fires of hell are real and eternal'. However, a subsequent Vatican 'clarification of the Pope's language' said that he had intended to 'reinforce what the Catechism affirmed about hell as a "state of eternal separation from God"', which was 'to be understood symbolically rather than physically'.[25]

The Catechism itself is illuminating. It begins by asserting unequivocally 'the sad and lamentable reality of eternal death also called hell'. This assertion is then qualified by statement that 'it is also true that God desires all men to be saved' and 'for God all things are possible'. Finally, it concludes: 'At the end of time the Kingdom of God will come in its fullness ... and God will be all in all.'[26]

7

Concepts of heaven

The 'three-decker universe'

There is no area of Christian doctrine where our understanding differs more from that of our forerunners than in the ways we think of heaven today. This was most clearly shown in Rudolf Bultmann's 1941 essay 'New Testament and Mythology', in which he highlighted the fact that the New Testament writers presupposed the cosmological picture of a 'three-decker universe', with the earth at its centre, heaven in the sky above the earth, and hell in an underworld below.

> New Testament writers presupposed the cosmological picture of a 'three-decker universe' with the earth at its centre, heaven in the sky above and hell in an underworld below

This understanding of reality is also the framework presupposed in the Christian creeds. Following the cosmological discoveries of the sixteenth century, however, it is a view of reality that is no longer seriously held by anyone.[1] Bultmann's thesis has generated decades of argument and discussion, initially summed up in the two-volume 1961 collection *Kerygma and Myth*. The essential truth of his thesis is indisputable, but still it has not been taken into account in liturgical rehearsals of the faith, nor in the language in which the Christian message is characteristically presented. Yet its implications for beliefs about life after death are profound.

The classic location of heaven in the sky

For the Christian Fathers, heaven was in the sky. Indeed, it *was* the sky. The Greek word *ouranos* means both sky and heaven, and

Concepts of heaven

for any person in the ancient world the two meanings would have been indistinguishable.[2] They remain very hard to distinguish in most European languages, as I discovered when lecturing on this topic in Germany. My opening comment that 'we no longer believe in a heaven in the sky' was initially untranslatable because *Himmel* in German means both sky and heaven. English is unusual in that during the seventeenth century the word 'heaven' was increasingly used with primary reference to the realm of the divine, while the word 'sky' came to be used as a descriptor of the upper atmosphere.

The patristic understanding of heaven as being located in the air above us can be vividly appreciated by reading the chapters in St Augustine's *City of God* in which he responded to objections that resurrected bodies, being heavier than air, could not stay up in the sky but would inevitably fall to earth. St Augustine pointed out that although iron is heavier than water, human skill can shape iron ships that stay afloat, so God's skill can shape us for life in the sky. Alternatively, we might be given powerful feathers like birds, or perhaps God would 'enable the perfect spirits of the blessed' to carry the weight of a human body into the sky just as immaterial angels are enabled to carry weights. He also argued that since the whole earth hangs in space without support, so too could our resurrected bodies.[3] Rufinus, in his early *Commentary on the Apostles' Creed*, argued on the basis of 1 Thessalonians 4.17 that we will be taken up to heaven on clouds.[4]

Not all the Fathers were troubled by such considerations, for in ancient Hebrew thought the floor of the sky was thought to be as solid as anything could be,[5] so the problem of falling to earth did not arise. Others thought not of a three-decker universe but of an earth surrounded by the heavenly spheres: Christians like Origen placed the 'good land', or *the* ultimate 'abiding place' of the blessed, above the 'spheres which surround the earth'.[6] But whatever view

> Almost all early Christian writers were confident that heaven was a literal place

they took, almost all early Christian writers were confident that heaven was a literal place.

This view of the world may help us understand why Christian leaders saw the discoveries of Copernicus and Galileo as a threat to their Christianity. This was not primarily an issue about astronomy; it was crucial for their faith in a heavenly destiny after death. It became impossible to think of heaven existing as a place in the upper atmosphere, or even in the heavenly spheres surrounding the earth. It is only when we appreciate this that we can understand why, in the seventeenth century, Blaise Pascal was terrified by the realization that the music of the heavenly spheres had been replaced by 'the eternal silence of those infinite spaces'.[7] From this time onwards, Christian parents have felt embarrassed when their children ask, 'Where is heaven?' To answer 'above the bright blue sky' is to evade a very real difficulty.

Perhaps I exaggerate the difficulty, however, because people are generally content to use language in different ways in different contexts. We still talk of sunrise and sunset even though we know intellectually that it is the earth that moves and not the sun. Similarly, many Christians unselfconsciously sing Easter and Ascension Day hymns which locate heaven in the sky; and as late as 1950 the bodily Assumption of Mary into the sky was made a *de fide* belief for the Roman Catholic Christian. Nevertheless, it remains the case that since the sixteenth century, educated Christians have found it hard to integrate their hope for heaven within their overall understanding of reality. A wide variety of ways of coping with this challenge have been made by Christian theology, and these form the focus of this chapter.

An eschatological heaven

Many New Testament scholars emphasize the eschatological hope of first-century thought, namely that God would bring history to a close, creating a new heaven and earth.

This understanding of heaven is perhaps closest to the traditional view. Since the time of Albert Schweitzer and Johannes Weiss, around the turn of the twentieth century, there has been a strong recovery of interest in the apocalyptic emphasis; this was later taken up into the systematic theology of Wolfhart Pannenberg and Jürgen Moltmann. Pannenberg insists that 'the basis on which the understanding of Jesus rests is always linked to the apocalyptic framework of Jesus' earthly life . . . if this framework is removed then the fundamental basis of faith is lost'.[8] For Moltmann, eschatology is 'the key to the whole of Christian faith'.[9] He looks forward to the transformation of the whole world and the whole future. For such writers, belief in the empty tomb and bodily resurrection of Jesus is central to faith because what happened to Jesus then will happen to us all at the universal resurrection of the dead at the end of time.

> The eschatological hope of first-century thought was that God would bring history to a close, creating a new heaven and earth

This theme is central to N. T. Wright's influential work *The Resurrection of the Son of God*; it is also spelt out particularly clearly in Andrew Chester's chapter on eschatology in *The Blackwell Companion to Modern Theology*. Chester argues that this way of thinking does full justice to the biblical stress on the psychosomatic unity of the whole person and our place within the created order. It enables one to dispense with the 'Greek' concept of the soul and accept as an absolute the 'Hebrew' understanding of the importance of embodiment to our personal identity. For Chester, the true Christian hope entails 'the recognition that the whole future and all time are set within God's control'.[10] This way of thinking takes absolutely seriously St Paul's thought that 'the universe itself is to be freed from the shackles of mortality and is to enter into the glorious liberty of the children of God'.[11]

Concepts of heaven

The virtue claimed for this way of thinking is that it places a physical understanding of the resurrection of Jesus at the centre of Christian thinking, and it takes with the utmost seriousness eschatological ideas that were undoubtedly present in the earliest structures of Christianity. However, this interpretation is by no means the only way in which the Christian hope is formulated within the New Testament. St Paul himself is far from consistent and his thought can be interpreted in many ways. A greater difficulty is that the apocalyptic picture of the first century is the only basis for such an expectation. Key elements in that understanding of reality are utterly different from our own. The most obvious is that early Christians initially expected that this would happen within their lifetime.[12] Another difficulty is that in New Testament times a recently created three-decker universe comprised the whole of reality and it was therefore not at all implausible to imagine that God would bring the existing structures to an end and create a new world for us. It is, of course, possible that millions of years hence the present universe may come to an end through some 'big crunch' analogous to the initial 'big bang'. Long before that, all life on our planet will have died out and our sun will have exploded as a red giant or a supernova. To imagine that at the end of time God will collect together all the molecules of every human being who has ever lived and raise them to new life in a newly created universe is a quite bewildering concept.

> To imagine that at the end of time God will collect together all the molecules of every human being and raise them to new life is a quite bewildering concept

When we note that champions of this position insist that this new creation will involve not only all humanity but the whole of creation including 'long extinct animals'[13] and even 'every blade of grass',[14] then the picture presented is even more implausible, and indeed impossible, given what we know about the way molecules are recycled within living systems.

A theocentric heaven

Colleen McDannell and Bernhard Lang, in *Heaven: A History*,[15] show that one way the Reformers responded to the Copernican revolution in astronomy was to place the whole emphasis of thinking about heaven into their understanding of God. If there was no longer any real place for a literal heaven 'above the bright blue sky', God himself would be our place. In the twentieth century this way of thinking was pushed to its limit by scholars who stressed the view expressed in 1 Timothy that God alone has immortality.[16] Karl Barth and Karl Rahner, arguably the most influential Protestant and Catholic thinkers of the twentieth century, adopted this course. Barth was insistent that we have only one life, which begins at birth and ends at death. This is our 'real and only life'; there can be 'no question of a continuation into an indefinite future of a somewhat altered life'. Rahner was equally clear: 'with death it's all over. Life is past, and it won't come again.' However, neither saw their respective positions as incompatible with belief in eternal life. For Barth, 'death will make our lives complete in God', while for Rahner, 'our emptiness will be filled in timeless eternity with the light of the divine spirit'.[17] Similarly, Paul Tillich insisted that 'Eternal life does not mean a continuation of temporal life after death.'[18]

The process philosopher Charles Hartshorne developed these ideas further. He argued that after death we will 'live on in the complete and infallible memory of God', and that:

> After death we will live on in the complete and infallible memory of God

> What we once were to him, less than that we can never be, for otherwise he himself as knowing us would lose something of his own reality... Death cannot be the destruction or even the fading of the book of one's life; it can only be the fixing of the concluding page. Death writes 'The End' but nothing further happens to the book either by addition or subtraction.[19]

Concepts of heaven

This view is echoed by David Edwards: 'God's memory of us will be more powerful and altogether better than our own memories', and because God remembers us, 'we will share in God's life and God's glory'.[20] According to Miguel de Unamuno, writing in the early twentieth century, to be remembered by God is 'to have my consciousness sustained by the Supreme consciousness'.[21]

In my earlier book, *Immortality or Extinction?*, I was highly critical of such positions.[22] Like John Hick, I argued that it seems to suggest that 'the state of being remembered constitutes as full and real an existence as the state of being alive'.[23] There is an important difference between being remembered, even by God, and continuing to exist as an independent subject. Even so, faced with the difficulty of articulating and defending belief in individual life after life, there is some attractiveness in these views. According to Peter Hamilton, the implication of such positions is that 'everything of any value in our life will be ... immortalized in God's supremely personal life'.[24] While this may offer less than a doctrine of personal immortality, it offers more than seeing death as extinction.

An eternal destiny

A theocentric heaven, in which God will be all in all, can also be seen as a way of making sense of ideas that run very deep in the Christian tradition. In the theology of the Orthodox Church there is a concept of our 'deification'. This is the idea that after death we will live in God as 'partakers of the divine nature'. We will share in the fullness of God's eternal life. In developing this position, Orthodoxy presupposes an understanding of God's eternity that is most characteristically associated with the sixth-century philosopher Boethius. He defined God's eternity as 'the total, complete, and simultaneous possession of unending life'.[25] For God, past, present

> God is outside time as well as outside space. At death we too pass from time into eternity

and future are all equally present. God is outside time as well as outside space. At death we too pass from time into eternity. As St Augustine put it, 'we shall rest in the Sabbath of eternal life ... in the repose which comes when time ceases'.[26]

> We shall rest in the Sabbath of eternal life ... in the repose which comes when time ceases

The essential timelessness of 'eternal life' means a completed life in which nothing further can happen. This is congruent with much Christian thinking about our future destiny. In the Catholic tradition it is 'eternal rest' (*requiem aeternam*) that we pray that the departed will experience after death. The night-time Compline prayer expresses a real attractiveness in the thought that 'We who are fatigued by the changes and chances of this fleeting world may repose upon thy eternal changelessness.' Consider also Cardinal Newman's famous prayer: 'May He support us all the day long, till the shades lengthen and the evening comes, and the busy world is hushed, and the fever of life is over, and our work is done. Then in His mercy may He give us a safe lodging, and a holy rest and peace at the last.'[27]

The communion of saints and the life of the world to come

The problem with belief in a timeless, unchanging existence after death is that nothing further can happen. This is different from 'the living hope' of the New Testament. The penitent thief asked Jesus to 'remember him'. Jesus' response offered far more than remembrance: 'Today you will be with me in Paradise' (Luke 23.43). What gives our lives meaning and purpose is living in fellowship with others and finding fulfilment in what we do. The credal belief in 'the communion of saints' implies a social heaven. The 'life of the world to come' implies further opportunity for new experiences.

> The 'life of the world to come' implies further opportunity for new experiences

Concepts of heaven

To the question, 'Where is heaven?' we can give no answer, not least because 'where' is a concept limited to our material universe. When his disciples asked a similar question Jesus reassured them: 'Set your troubled hearts at rest. Trust in God always; trust also in me. There are many dwelling-places in my Father's house; if it were not so I should have told you' (John 14.1–2).

Immortality and resurrection

We saw in Chapter 2 that the Christian tradition has posited a two-stage understanding of our future destiny, with the immortality of the soul being followed in due course by resurrection of the body. Both seem important for a fully personal understanding of life after death: the immortality of the soul to ensure continuity between this life and the next, and the resurrection of the body to ensure that the soul has a means of expression and activity.

In Catholic Christianity the bridging stage of existence is covered by its belief in the survival of the soul. Pope John Paul II's encyclical *Man's Condition After Death* makes this clear: 'The Church affirms that a spiritual element survives and subsists after death, an element endued with consciousness and will, so that "the human self" subsists, though deprived for the present of the complement of its body.'[28]

John Hick suggested that at death our consciousness temporarily enters a mind-dependent world, akin to that as described in *The Tibetan Book of the Dead*. A mind-dependent world would be a kind of dream environment built out of our memories and desires and thereby revealing to us their true nature. This would provide an opportunity for life-review, self-revelation and self-assessment, and enable us to learn from our experiences of earthly life. It would also provide opportunity for 'meeting' through telepathic rapport with deceased relatives and friends and an enhanced awareness of the divine. This idea would be congruent not only with Christian ideas of the immortality of the soul but also with Hindu and

Concepts of heaven

Buddhist speculations of a '*bardo*' world of thought alone which would immediately follow our earthly existence. Neither the Eastern religions nor Christianity see this as our permanent destiny, but as a temporary stage for reflection before reincarnation, rebirth or resurrection. This thought corresponds to the notion deeply rooted in Christianity that the persistence of the soul in a disembodied state would be unnatural to it. It must, in St Paul's words, be 'clothed upon' by a new body if the full person is truly to live again.

John Hick contributed to thought about resurrection through his 'replica' theory. He suggested that if God were to create a 'replica' of each of us, possessing sufficient correspondence of characteristics with our present bodies and sufficient continuity of memory with our present consciousness, then we could validly claim belief in resurrection.[29]

The resurrection of Jesus matters to Christians because in his risen body we see the exemplification of this hope. His risen body was clearly sufficiently akin to his earthly body for the disciples usually to recognize him, while at the same time it was free from the limitations of a mortal existence and led to the disciples' confidence that Jesus had truly triumphed over death and that they too would share in this risen life.

The Christian hope of immortality and resurrection, as thus articulated, is coherent within itself and is grounded in people's experience of God, both within the Christian community and in the wider religious experience of the human race.

> The Christian hope of immortality and resurrection is coherent within itself and is grounded in people's experience of God

A strong, living relationship with God includes trusting in the reality of that fellowship against the forces of death. To many this may seem an exceedingly frail foundation on which to build the momentous claim that there is life after death. But for those to whom God is a reality, no basis could be more secure.

Notes

1 Making sense of death

1 David Hume, *On Religion* (London: Fontana, 1963), pp. 267–8.
2 Genesis 35.18.
3 Eric Rust, *Nature and Man in Biblical Thought* (Cambridge: Lutterworth Press, 1953), p. 104.
4 Psalms 49.12; 90.5; 103.15.
5 Job 14.1–19.
6 Ecclesiastes 3.12; 5.18; 9.9–10.
7 Nick Spencer, *Darwin and God* (London: SPCK, 2009), p. 45.
8 In A. Linzey and D. Yamamoto, *Animals on the Agenda* (London: SCM Press, 1998).
9 St Thomas Aquinas, *Summa Theologiae* 1a.89.1 (London: Eyre and Spottiswoode, 1968), p. 143.
10 Linda Badham, 'A naturalistic case for extinction', in Paul and Linda Badham (eds), *Death and Immortality in the Religions of the World* (St Paul, MN: Paragon House, 1987), p. 163.
11 *The Lancet*, 26 January 1980, Vol. 1, p. 167.
12 L. Wittgenstein, *Tractatus Logico-Philosophicus* 6.431 and 61411, cited in A. Flew and A. MacIntyre (eds), *New Essays in Philosophical Theology* (London: SCM Press, 1963), p. 272.
13 Flew and MacIntyre, *New Essays*, p. 269.
14 Genesis 6.3.
15 Information on Jeanne Calment from Wikipedia.
16 Guy Brown, *The Living End* (London: Macmillan, 2008), pp. 27–30.
17 *The Times*, 1 September 2012.
18 Brown, *Living End*, pp. 74 and 278.
19 Information from Wikipedia and World Crunch; *Le Monde*, 25 October 2011.
20 Douglas Davies, *A Brief History of Death* (Oxford: Blackwell, 2005), p. 205.

21 Michael Young and Lesley Cullen, *A Good Death; Conversations with East Londoners* (London: Routledge, 1996), p. 36.
22 Francis Crick, *Of Molecules and Men* (Seattle, WA: University of Washington Press, 1966), p. 99.

2 Making sense of immortality

1 Anton van der Valle, *From Darkness to the Dawn* (London: SCM Press, 1984), p. 120.
2 Bede, *A History of the English Church*, Book 2, Chapter 13.
3 When I first affirmed this as a doctoral student my supervisor, Professor John Hick, warned that such an assertion would require full documentation. Six months later, backed by 17 pages of references, the sentence was allowed to stand.
4 R. Lawler, D. W. Wuerl and T. C. Lawler, *The Teaching of Christ: A Catholic Catechism for Adults* (Veritas, 1976), p. 544.
5 Rufinus, *Commentary on the Apostles' Creed*, paras 42 and 43; Revelation 20.13; Augustine, *City of God*, 22.20.
6 *Scientific American*, 30 November 2007.
7 John Macquarrie, *The Christian Hope* (London: Mowbray, 1978), p. 117.
8 A. J. Ayer, *The Central Questions of Philosophy* (Harmondsworth: Penguin, 1976), p. 133.
9 Ayer, *Central Questions*, p. 124.
10 R. Descartes, *Discourse on Method* (Harmondsworth: Penguin, 1968), p. 159.
11 Baron d'Holbach, cited in the *Journal of the Philosophical Society of Great Britain*, Vol. 14 (no date), p. 145.
12 Jacques Monod, *Chance and Necessity* (New York: Vintage, 1971), pp. 30–1.
13 St Paul, in 1 Corinthians 2.14.
14 Peter and Elizabeth Fenwick, in Paul Badham and Paul Ballard (eds), *Facing Death* (Cardiff: University of Wales Press, 1996); and Mark Fox, *Religion, Spirituality and the Near-death Experience* (London: Routledge, 2003).
15 John Hick, *Death and Eternal Life* (London: Collins, 1976), p. 47.

16 Richard Swinburne, *Is There a God?* (Oxford: Oxford University Press, 1996), p. 77.
17 Richard Swinburne, *The Evolution of the Soul* (Oxford: Oxford University Press, 1986), pp. 1–2.
18 Keith Ward, *The Battle for the Soul* (London: Hodder and Stoughton, 1985), pp. 149–50.
19 Church of England Doctrine Commission, *Doctrine in the Church of England* (London: SPCK, 1938, reprinted 1962), p. 207.
20 *Catechism of the Catholic Church* (London: Chapman, 1994), pp. 83, 227.
21 Church of England Doctrine Commission, *The Mystery of Salvation* (London: Church House Publishing, 1996), pp. 10–11, 191–2.
22 Stuart Brown, *Philosophy of Religion* (London: Routledge, 2001).
23 David Cockburn, *An Introduction to the Philosophy of Mind* (London: Palgrave, 2001).

3 The religious context of belief in a future life

1 Stephen Hawking, *A Brief History of Time* (London: Bantam Press, 1988), p. 127; John Leslie, *Universes* (London: Routledge, 1989), pp. 29, 37, 3, 28.
2 Antony Flew, *There is a God: How the World's Most Notorious Atheist Changed his Mind* (New York: HarperOne, 2009).
3 Antony Flew, 'My pilgrimage from atheism to theism'. Online at: <www.biola.edu/antonyflew/flew-interview.pdf>. Also see *Philosophia Christi*, Winter 2005.
4 Antony Flew, in Stan Wallace, *Does God Exist? The Craig–Flew Debate* (Aldershot: Ashgate, 2003), p. 190.
5 Flew, 'My pilgrimage'.
6 Sandra Menssen and Thomas Sullivan, *The Agnostic Inquirer* (Grand Rapids, MI: Eerdmans, 2007), p. xi.
7 Kai Nielsen, *Contemporary Critiques of Religion* (London: Macmillan, 1971), p. 19; and 'Foreword' to K. Parsons, *God and the Burden of Proof* (New York: Prometheus, 1989), p. 7.
8 Richard Purtill, 'The Current State of Arguments for the Existence of God', *Review and Expositor*, Vol. 82 (1985).

9 Graham Oppy and Nick Trakakis (eds) *The History of Western Philosophy of Religion* (Durham: Acumen, 2009), Vol. 5, p. 1.
10 Basil Mitchell, *The Justification of Religious Belief* (Oxford: Oxford University Press, 1982).
11 M. B. Forman (ed), *The Letters of John Keats* (Oxford: Oxford University Press, 1952), pp. 344–5.
12 Don Cupitt, *The Debate about Christ* (London: SCM Press, 1979), p. 17.
13 Isaiah 49.6–15; 40.11–15.
14 Genesis 15.12–17; 17.1–8; Exodus 3.1–6; 1 Samuel 3.1–9; Isaiah 6.1–8.
15 Mark 1.22; 9.2–10; 1 Corinthians 15.3–8.
16 Michael Van Horn, *Within my Heart*, PhD thesis (Lampeter: University of Wales, 2001).
17 Xinzhong Yao and Paul Badham, *Religious Experience in Contemporary China* (Cardiff: University of Wales Press, 2007), p. 185.
18 Olga Pupynin and Simon Brodbeck, *Religious Experience in London*, occasional paper (Lampeter: Religious Experience Research Centre, 2001).
19 Yen-Zen Tsai, *Religious Experience Survey in Taiwan* (Taiwan: National Chengchi University, 2009), question 9.
20 Cafer Yaran, 'Religious experience in contemporary Turkey', *Modern Believing*, Vol. 51, No. 4 (October 2010), p. 49.
21 Jonathan Robinson, 'Religious experience in Tamil Nadu', *Modern Believing*, Vol. 50, No. 2 (April 2009).
22 For the full development of this argument see Paul Badham, *Christian Beliefs About Life after Death* (London: Macmillan, 1976).
23 Wheeler Robinson, *Inspiration and Revelation in the Old Testament* (Oxford: Oxford University Press, 1962), p. 103.

4 A historical argument for belief in the resurrection of Jesus

1 William James, *The Varieties of Religious Experience*, Gifford Lectures, Edinburgh 1901–2 (1902; London: Collins, 1963).
2 Kathy Ehrensperger, in Leslie and Paul Badham, *Verdict on Jesus* (London: SPCK, 2010), pp. 244–50.

Notes to pages 38–48

3 Cf. Matthew 28.19.
4 Tacitus, *Annals*, 15/442–6, in H. M. Gwatkin, *Selections from Early Christian Writers* (London: Macmillan, 1920), p. 3; cf. J. Stevenson, *A New Eusebius* (London: SPCK, 1963), p. 2.
5 Robert Wilken, *The Christians as the Romans Saw Them* (New Haven and London: Yale University Press, 1984), p. 45.
6 Translation adapted from Gwatkin, *Selections*, p. 20, and Stevenson, *A New Eusebius*, p. 14, also p. 15 note 7.
7 Both cited from Wilken, *Christians*, p. 105.
8 Adolf Harnack, *What is Christianity?* (1901; London: Benn, 1958), pp. 120–1.
9 St Athanasius, *On the Incarnation* (London: Mowbray, 1963), pp. 57–9.
10 'Trajan's reply to Pliny', in Stevenson, *A New Eusebius*, p. 16.
11 A. Droge and J. Tabor, *A Noble Death* (San Francisco: Harper, 1992), p. 154.
12 Wilken, *Christians*, p. 98.
13 C. F. Evans, *Resurrection and the New Testament* (London: SCM Press, 1970), p. 64.
14 D. E. Nineham, *Historicity and Chronology in the New Testament*, Theological Collections No. 6 (London: SPCK, 1965), p. 127.
15 Church of England Doctrine Commission, *Doctrine in the Church of England* (London: SPCK, 1938 reprinted 1962), pp. 83–8.
16 Paul Badham, *The Contemporary Challenge of Modernist Theology* (Cardiff: University of Wales Press, 1998), Chapters 8 and 9.

5 The evidential and religious value of near-death experiences

1 Figures from Peter and Elizabeth Fenwick, 'The near-death experience', in Paul Badham and Paul Ballard (eds) *Facing Death* (Cardiff: University of Wales Press, 1996).
2 Paul and Linda Badham, *Immortality or Extinction?* (London: SPCK, 1984), p. 85.
3 Michael Marsh, *Out-of-Body and Near-Death Experiences* (Oxford: Oxford University Press, 2010).

4 Karlis Osis and Erlendur Haraldsson, *At the Hour of Death* (New York: Avon, 1997).
5 *Church Times*, 13 September 2002, p. 16.
6 Michael Sabom, *Light and Death* (Michigan: Zondervan, 1998), p. 41 See also online: <www.near-death.com/reynolds.html> and <www.ndeweb.com/wildcard/>.
7 *The Day I Died*, BBC (2002), also available on the internet.
8 Janice Holden, 'Foreword', in Mahendra Perera, Karuppian Jagadheesan and Anthony Peake (eds), *Making Sense of Near-death Experiences* (London: Jessica Kingsley, 2012).
9 *At the Hour of Death*, BBC Everyman series (March 1982).
10 Susan Blackmore, *Dying to Live: Science and the Near-Death Experience* (London: Grafton, 1993), pp. 114–15.
11 Penny Sartori, *Near-Death Experiences of Hospitalized Intensive Care Patients* (Lewiston, NY: Mellen, 2008), pp. 212–15.
12 Gregory Shushan, *Conceptions of the Afterlife in Early Civilizations* (London and New York: Continuum, 2009).
13 *Zohar*, Vol. 2, p. 307, cited in M. Cox-Chapman, *Visions of Death: The Near-death Experience* (London: Hale, 1996), p. 139.
14 *The Tibetan Book of the Dead: or, the After-Death Experiences on the Bardo Plane, according to Lama Kazi Dawa-Samdup's English Rendering*, ed. W. Y. Evans-Wentz (1927; Oxford: Oxford University Press, 1957), pp. 98, 101.
15 Sogyal Rinpoche, *The Tibetan Book of Living and Dying* (London: Routledge, 1992), pp. 330–6.
16 Plato, *The Republic*, tr. H. D. P. Lee (Harmondsworth: Penguin, 1955), Part 11, Section 3, p. 394.
17 Karen Armstrong, *A History of God* (London: Heinemann, 1993), p. 163; cited from Jalal al-Din Suyiti, al-itqan fi'ulum al-aq'ran as quoted by Maxime Rodinson, *Muhammad* (London: Allen Lane, 1971), p. 74.
18 See discussion in Karen Armstrong, *Muhammad* (London: Gollancz, 1991), pp. 138–42.
19 2 Corinthians 12.2–5.
20 2 Corinthians 12.7.

21 St John of the Cross, *The Dark Night of the Soul*, tr. K. Reinhardt (London: Constable, 1957), Book 2, Chapter 24, p. 84.
22 St John of the Cross, *Poems*, tr. R. Campbell (Harmondsworth: Penguin, 1960), p. 51; all from 47 to 57 are relevant. That secular love poems of that time use the phrase 'dying that I do not die' as a sexual metaphor does not prevent us from supposing that St John was using the expression in its primary sense.
23 *Tibetan Book of the Dead*, p. 94.
24 A. J. Ayer, 'What I saw when I was dead', in Paul Edwards (ed.), *Immortality* (New York: Macmillan, 1992).
25 Bukkyo Dendo Kyokai, *The Teaching of Buddha* (Tokyo: Buddhist Promoting Foundation, 1980), p. 218, quoting from *Amitayurdhyana-sutra*.
26 Eben Alexander, *Proof of Heaven: A Neurosurgeon's Journey into the Afterlife* (London: Piatkus, 2012).

6 Moral and religious arguments against belief in hell

1 Collated from Matthew 25.32, 34, 46 and Revelation 20.10; 21.8.
2 Augustine, *City of God*, 22.11; Minucius Felix, *Octavius*, Ch. 35; Basil, *Letter 8*; Lactantius, *Divine Institutes*, 7.21; Justin, *First Apology*, 8.
3 Hippolytus, *Treatise of Christ and Anti-Christ*, Ch. 65.
4 Tertullian, *De Spectaculis*, Ch. 30, cited in W. R. Alger, *The Destiny of the Soul* (1860; New York: Greenwood Press, 1968), p. 13.
5 P. Lombard, *Sentences*, 4.50.7, cited in P. Dearmer, *The Legend of Hell* (London: Cassell, 1929), p. 34.
6 St Thomas Aquinas, *Summa Theologiae*, 3.94.1, cited in A. Flew, *God and Philosophy* (London: Hutchinson, 1966), p. 57.
7 H. J. D. Denzinger, *The Church Teaches: Documents of the Church in English Translation* (Freiburg: Herder, 1965), p. 165.
8 Alger, *Destiny of the Soul*, p. 515.
9 Dearmer, *Legend of Hell*, p. 25.
10 Cf. F. W. Farrer, *Eternal Hope* (1878; London: Macmillan, 1912), Chapter 3; G. Rowell, *Hell and the Victorians* (London: Clarendon Press, 1974), Chapter 2.
11 D. Cupitt, *Crisis of Moral Authority* (Cambridge: Lutterworth Press, 1972), p. 77.

12 Ian Bradley, *The Call to Seriousness* (London: Jonathan Cape, 1976), p. 188.
13 For full documentation of this see Rowell, *Hell and the Victorians*.
14 F. D. E. Schleiermacher, *The Christian Faith* (1830; Edinburgh: T & T Clark, 1960), pp. 709ff.
15 St Thomas Aquinas, *Summa Theologia*, 3.94.1.
16 F. D. Maurice, *Theological Essays* (1853; London: Macmillan, 1871), p. 14.
17 Cited in F. Higham, *F. D. Maurice* (London: SCM Press, 1947), p. 93.
18 H. B. Wilson, 'The National Church', in B. Jowett (ed.), *Essays and Reviews* (London: Parker, 1960), p. 206.
19 Evangelical Alliance, *The Nature of Hell* (London: Acute, 2000), p. 132.
20 J. A. Motyer, *After Death* (London: Hodder, 1965), pp. 27, 35, 36, 38, 40, 46, 47.
21 Isaiah 55.9.
22 J. S. Mill, *An Examination of Sir William Hamilton's Philosophy* (Boston, MA: William Spencer, 1866), p. 103.
23 Pope John Paul II, *Sign of Contradiction* (London: Hodder, 1980), p. 180.
24 Pope John Paul II, *Redemptor Hominis*, encyclical letter (1979), para. 14.
25 *The Times*, 27 March 2007.
26 *Catechism of the Catholic Church* (London: Chapman, 1994), pp. 240–1.

7 Concepts of heaven

1 R. Bultmann, 'New Testament and mythology', in H. W. Bartsch (ed.), *Kerygma and Myth* (New York: Harper Torchbooks, 1961), pp. 1–4.
2 Paul Badham, *Christian Beliefs About Life after Death* (London: Macmillan, 1976), p. 59.
3 Augustine, *City of God*, 13.18; 22.4; 22.11.
4 Rufinus, *Commentary on the Apostles' Creed*, para. 46.
5 W. Eichrodt, *Theology of the Old Testament* (London: SCM Press, 1967), Vol. 2, p. 93.
6 Origen, *First Principles*, 2.11; 6–7.
7 Blaise Pascal, *Pensées*, Section 2, No. 206.

8. C. F. D. Moule (ed.), *The Significance of the Message of the Resurrection of Jesus Christ* (London: SCM Press, 1968), p. 130, summarizing W. Pannenberg, *Jesus: God and Man* (London: SCM Press, 1968), pp. 63–73.
9. A. Chester, 'Eschatology', in G. Jones (ed.), *The Blackwell Companion to Modern Theology* (Oxford: Blackwell, 2004), p. 251, summarizing J. Moltmann, *Theology of Hope*.
10. Chester, 'Eschatology', p. 256.
11. Romans 8.21.
12. 1 Thessalonians 4.15.
13. John Macquarrie, *The Christian Hope* (London: Mowbray, 1978), p. 128.
14. N. Berdyaev, *The Destiny of Man* (London: Geoffrey Bles, 1955), p. 294.
15. Colleen McDannell and Bernhard Lang, *Heaven: A History* (New York: Vintage, 1990).
16. 1 Timothy 6.16.
17. McDannell and Lang, *Heaven*, pp. 342–3.
18. Paul Tillich, *Systematic Theology* (Welwyn: Nisbet, 1968), Vol. 3, p. 437.
19. Cited in John Hick, *Death and Eternal Life* (London: Collins, 1976), p. 218.
20. David Edwards, *The Last Things Now* (London: SCM Press, 1969), p. 89.
21. M. de Unamuno, *The Tragic Sense of Life* (1912; London: Fontana, 1967), p. 154.
22. Paul and Linda Badham, *Immortality or Extinction?* (London: SPCK, 1984), pp. 30–5.
23. Hick, *Death and Eternal Life*, p. 219.
24. Peter Hamilton, *The Living God and the Modern World* (London: Hodder, 1967), pp. 108–41, cited in Edwards, *Last Things Now*, p. 92.
25. Boethius, *The Consolation of Philosophy*, V.6.
26. St Augustine, *Confessions*, 13:36–37 (Harmondsworth: Penguin, 1961), p. 346.
27. *Prayers and Hymns of John Henry Newman* (CatholiCity.com © 1996–2012, The Mary Foundation).
28. J. Neuner and J. Dupuis, *The Christian Faith in the Doctrinal Documents of the Catholic Church* (London: Collins, 1983), p. 691.
29. Hick, *Death and Eternal Life*, pp. 278–90.

www.ingramcontent.com/pod-product-compliance
Lightning Source LLC
Chambersburg PA
CBHW071218070526
44584CB00019B/3066